CONTENTS

KEY FACTS

TORT

CHRIS TURNER

Hodder & Stoughton

A MEMBER OF THE HODDER HEADLINE GROUP

Orders: please contact Bookpoint Ltd, 130 Milton Park, Abingdon, Oxon OX14 4SB.
Telephone: (44) 01235 827720. Fax: (44) 01235 400454. Lines are open from 9.00–6.00,
Monday to Saturday, with a 24-hour message answering service.
You can also order through our website www.hodderheadline.co.uk

British Library Cataloguing in Publication Data
A catalogue record for this title is available from The British Library.

ISBN 0 340 801824

First published 2001
Impression number   10 9 8 7 6 5 4 3
Year   2005 2004 2003

Cover design by Stewart Larking
Typeset by Transet Limited, Coventry, England.
Printed in Great Britain for Hodder & Stoughton Educational, a division of Hodder Headline,
338 Euston Road, London NW1 3BH by Cox & Wyman Ltd, Reading, Berkshire.

PREFACE

The Key Facts series is designed to give a clear view of each subject. This will be useful to students when tackling new topics and is invaluable as a revision aid. Most chapters open with an outline in diagram form of the points covered in that chapter. The points are then developed in list form to make learning easier. Supporting cases are given throughout by name and for some complex areas the facts of cases are given to reinforce the point being made.

The topics covered for the Law of Torts are suitable for students on a variety of courses, including first year degree and foundation courses in law as well as ILEX courses at Part 1 and Part 2, and also A Level and certain elements of AS Level. They include all of the main areas of any mainstream Law of Torts syllabuses. The only slight omission for the sake of space is the economic torts. The Law of Torts is an exciting and ever expanding area and every effort has been made to include the complexities of the subject.

The law is as I believe it to be on 1st August 2001.

CHAPTER 1

THE NATURE OF TORTIOUS LIABILITY

1.1 GENERAL PRINCIPLES OF TORTIOUS LIABILITY

1.1.1 The character of tort

1. The word tort comes from the French meaning 'wrong'.
2. Tort concerns civil wrongs leading to possible compensation.
3. A common definition is: 'Tortious liability arises from the breach of a duty primarily fixed by law; such duty is towards persons generally and its breach is redressable by an action for unliquidated damages.' (Winfield)
4. Character is dictated by historical background, so better definition is: 'subject to statutory intervention, a tort is a wrong which in former times would have been remediable by one of the actions for trespass (for direct wrongs) or trespass upon the case (for indirect wrongs)' (Cooke) – so should refer to a law of torts.
5. The standard modern model is as follows: the defendant's act or omission causes damage to the claimant through the fault of the defendant, and damage is of a type which attracts liability in law.
6. However, there are complications:
   a) strict liability torts do not require faults to be proved;
   b) the type of damage caused may not give rise to liability (*damnum sine injuria*);
   c) some conduct results in liability even without damage (*injuria sine damno*).

1.1.2 The aims of tort

1. There are two principal objectives in tort: deterrence and compensation.

a) **Deterrence** operates more on a market than an individual basis – the idea is to reduce the cost of accidents.
b) **Compensation** – the purpose of damages is to put the victim in the same position as if tort did not occur (reliance loss).

2. A key question is whether the system adequately compensates victims.

3. Points to consider:
- only those who can show fault can be compensated;
- both Pearson and Woolf report identified delay and costs as major drawbacks;
- reductions in value of compensation: pressure is on the claimant to settle – usual for two-third to three-quarters;
- unpredictability;
- no point suing 'a man of straw' – exceptions are third party insurance under Road Traffic Acts; vicarious liability; Employer's Liability (Compulsory Insurance) Act 1969;
- the system discourages claims: only one in ten potential personal injury claims are pursued;
- the effect of the Woolf reforms on encouraging or deterring claims.

1.1.3 Alternative methods of compensation

1. These were considered as early as Royal Commission on Civil Liability and Compensation for Personal Injury (Pearson Commission) 1978.

2. The Commission was the follow-up to the Thalidomide scandal.

3. The Commission did not recommend an end to the tort system in personal injury, but did recommend a partial no-fault system.

4. New Zealand operates such a scheme: benefits up to 80% of earnings; limited lump sum amounts in permanent disability – 1982 reforms found no one in favour of returning to fault system.

5. Public insurance is one alternative – Pearson showed that the cost of obtaining tort compensation is much higher than the cost of administering the Social Security system.
6. Private insurance – too expensive for many people, and not within British culture.
7. Compensation from public schemes, e.g. Criminal Injuries Compensation Scheme, Motor Insurance Bureau, if applicable.

1.1.4 The interests the law of torts protects

1. It is possible to classify torts according to type of interest.
2. These include the following.
   a) Personal Security:
      - original trespass actions, e.g. battery, etc.;
      - more recently includes negligence, e.g. medical negligence;
      - and psychiatric extensions, e.g. nervous shock.
   b) Property:
      - interests in land protected by trespass, nuisance, (*Rylands v Fletcher* (1868));
      - interests in chattels by trespass, conversion, statute.
   c) Reputation:
      - an extension of personal security;
      - protected by defamation, malicious falsehood, etc.
   d) Economic loss:
      - much more controversial and problematic;
      - is limited because of the difficulty of distinguishing between lawful and unlawful business activities;
      - economic torts associated with competing activities of trade unions and businesses, e.g. procuring a breach of contract;
      - the law also recognises an action for economic loss caused by a negligently made statement;
      - but not for pure economic loss caused by an action.

1.1.5 Tort and mental states

1. There are three possible states of mind relevant to liability in tort, as listed below.

2. a) Malice:
   - improper motive, generally has no relevance in tort (*Bradford Corporation v Pickles* (1895));
   - but there are two exceptions:
     (i) where malice is an ingredient, e.g. malicious prosecution;
     (ii) where malice is an unreasonable act, as in nuisance – (*Christie v Davey* (1893)).

   b) Intention. Three possible groups:
   - torts deriving from the writ of trespass, e.g. assault;
   - fraud – defendant makes statement knowing it is untrue;
   - conspiracy – where claimant can show that the prime purpose of the conspirators is to harm him.

   c) Negligence:
   - a major tort in its own right, but also indicative of an objective standard imposed by law;
   - liability results from falling below the set standard;
   - the consequences of applying negligence as test of liability are that victims unable to show fault go uncompensated, and process of investigating facts needed to prove fault are costly and prohibitive.

1.1.6 Relationships with other areas of law

1. With crime.
   a) Dual liability is possible, but distinctions include:
   - the parties, e.g. the state's involvement in crime;
   - the outcome, e.g. liability as opposed to punishment;
   - terminology and procedural differences;
   - the standard of proof.

b) But they are not always so different, e.g. the right of the court to impose sanctions in medieval trespass actions.

2. With contract.

a) Duties in tort are imposed by law and apply generally, but contract duties are agreed by the parties and apply to them only.

b) Statute does now impose many contractual duties irrespective of the will of the parties.

c) There are potential overlaps, e.g. negligence and breach of implied conditions.

d) Difficulties are created both by the exceptions to the privity rules in contract, and by the tort action for economic loss, which blur the distinctions between the two areas.

e) Sometimes a claimant has a choice in which area to sue, e.g. in contract for private medicine where there is negligence.

1.1.7 The effects of the Human Rights Act 1998

1. This can have a major impact on many areas of law, not just tort.

2. The Act gives statutory effect to, and incorporates into English law, the European Convention of Human Rights.

3. Judges therefore have a new role as watchdogs of the Covention.

4. The Act demands all primary and secondary legislation to be interpreted to be compatible with provisions of the Convention.

5. Many Convention Articles are appropriate to the law of torts:

- Article 2 – the right to life (appropriate to medical torts);
- Article 3 – freedom from torture, inhuman or degrading treatment (trespass to the person);
- Article 4 – freedom from slavery;
- Article 5 – the right to liberty apart from lawful arrest;

- Article 8 – the right to respect for private and family life, home and correspondence (defamation, trespass, nuisance);
- Article 9 – freedom of thought, conscience and religion (defamation, unlawful arrest);
- Article 10 – freedom of expression (defamation).

6. The UK has faced many claims in the European Court of Human Rights and has a worse record than many other signatories.

1.2 FAULT AND NO-FAULT LIABILITY

1. Fault liability is unfair to claimants, because of difficulty of proof and evidence, and because victims of publicised events are advantaged.
2. It is unfair on defendants because there is no way of accounting for degree of culpability.
3. It is unfair on society generally because it creates classes of victims who can be compensated and classes that cannot.
4. It is also depends heavily on policy, so is arbitrary.
5. It is justified both for punishing wrongdoers and deterrent value.
6. Pearson has advocated no-fault schemes – two no-fault medical negligence bills since, but neither was accepted.

1.3 JOINT AND SEVERAL TORTFEASORS

1.3.1 Joint and several liability

1. Liability is straightforward, with a single act causing loss or injury.
2. Often more than one breach of duty or more than one act causes the damage, and liability may be independent, or joint, or several.
3. Independent liability is straightforward:

- two separate tortfeasers cause damage through separate torts;
- damage is separate, so each tortfeaser is liable for the particular damage caused.

4. Joint liability can arise in a number of different ways.

- All tortfeasers commit the same tortious act, often with a shared purpose (*Brooke v Bool* (1928)).
- If vicarious liability applies both employer and employee are jointly liable though only one would be sued – (sometimes tortfeasers are joined, e.g. in medical negligence).
- In non-delegable duties a person hiring an independent contractor causing the damage can be jointly liable.
- Where one person authorises the tort of another.
- Where the tort is committed by one member of a partnership each partner is jointly liable, but, since the damage comes from one tort, the claimant can only claim one lot of damages.

5. Several liability involves two separate tortfeasers causing the same damage through coincidental, independent acts:

- claimant chooses who to sue – usually the one with money;
- since there is only one lot of damage claimant can only recover once.

6. The practical result of the distinction between joint and several is that release of liability to a joint tortfeaser releases the others, while release to a several tortfeaser will not

1.3.2 Contributions between tortfeasers

1. Now governed by the Civil Liability (Contribution) Act 1978.
2. The basic proposition is in s1: 'any person liable in respect of any damage suffered by another person may recover a contribution from any other person liable in respect of the same damage (whether jointly liable with him or otherwise)'.
3. The person seeking a contribution must be actually or hypothetically liable.

4. Applies to any type of action, and wrongdoer's liability to claimant need not be based on breach of the same obligation – s6(1).
5. By s2(1) the amount of contribution is that which is 'just and equitable having regard to the extent of that person's responsibility for the damage...' (*Fitzgerald v Lane* (1988)).
6. By s1(2) a settlement by one tortfeaser does not remove his right to claim a contribution from the other, whether or not he himself was actually liable to the claimant (changing the old law where D1 could only claim from D2 if he could prove D2 was liable).
7. If a claimant's action against a person from whom contribution is sought is time barred, this does not prevent recovery of a contribution unless a two-year limitation period in s1(3) has expired.

1.4 GENERAL DEFENCES

1.4.1. Introduction

1. Defences can be both specific and general.
2. Some torts, e.g. defamation, have a range of specific defences.
3. Many defences, e.g. those in negligence, apply generally.
4. Most provide a total defence by showing the defendant is not at fault, others provide a partial defence only.

1.4.2 Volenti non fit injuria (consent)

1. This means no injury is done to one who voluntarily accepts a risk.
2. It does not apply where the claimant only knew of the existence of the risk rather than understanding it (*Stermer v Lawson* (1977)).
3. Nor does it apply where the claimant is forced to accept the risk (*Smith v Baker* (1891)).
4. It commonly applies in sporting situations if physical harm is likely (*Simms v Leigh RFC* (1969)) and (*Condon v Basi* (1985)).

5. It is important in the medical context (*Sidaway v Governors of Bethlem Royal Hospital* (1985)) where one issue is whether or not there is a requirement of informed consent.
6. It occasionally applies in certain employment situations (*Gledhill v Liverpool Abattoir Co. Ltd* (1957)).

1.4.3 Inevitable accident

1. A defendant is never liable for a pure accident.
2. Pure accident means one beyond the defendant's control (*Stanley v Powell* (1891)).

1.4.4 Act of God

1. Concerns extreme weather conditions.
2. However, they must be unforeseeable condition, not merely bad weather (*Nichols v Marsland* (1876)).

1.4.5 Self-defence

1. Everybody is entitled to defend himself.
2. But only by using reasonable force (*Lane v Holloway* (1968)).

1.4.6 Statutory authority

No liability if act authorised (*Vaughan v Taff Vale Railway* (1928)).

1.4.7 Illegality (ex turpi causa non oritur actio)

1. A defendant can avoid liability where the claimant suffers the harm while engaged in an illegal act (*Ashton v Turner* (1981)).
2. However, see more recently (*Revill v Newbury* (1996)).

1.4.8 Necessity

1. Applies if an act is done to avoid worse damage (*Watt v Herts. C.C.* (1954)).

2. Saving life is an obvious example (*Leigh v Gladstone* (1909)).

1.4.9 Contributory negligence

1. Originally this was a complete defence, but now governed by the Law Reform (Contributory Negligence) Act 1945 and partial only.
2. The effect is to reduce the claimant's damages where (s)he has contributed to his/her own harm (*Sayers v Harlow DC* (1958)).
3. It is now commonplace when accepting lifts from drunk drivers (*Stinton v Stinton* (1993)) or failing to wear crash helmets while a passenger on a motorbike (*O'Connell v Jackson* (1972)), or failing to wear a seat belt (*Froom v Butcher* (1976)).
4. It is not necessary to show that the claimant owed a duty of care, merely that (s)he failed to take care in all the circumstances.
5. However, causation must always be proved – the claimant's act in fact helped cause the damage suffered (*Woods v Davidson* (1930)).

CHAPTER 2

NEGLIGENCE

Lord Atkin's test in *Donoghue v Stephenson*

The neighbour principle: take reasonable care to avoid acts or omissions that would reasonably foreseeably injure a person so closely affected that you should have them in your contemplation.

Lord Wilberforce's two-part test in *Anns v Merton LBC*
- Is there sufficient proximity between claimant and defendant to impose a duty?
- Is there any reason of policy not to impose duty?

Overruled in (*Murphy v Brentwood DC*) because:
- duty too general based on policy alone;
- gave judges too much power.

Duty of care

Caparo v Dickman three-part test
- Reasonable foreseeability (*Fardon v Harcourt-Rivington*).
- Proximity (*Hill v Chief Constable of West Yorkshire*).
- Fair and reasonable to impose a duty (*Ephraim v Newham L.B.C.*).

The role of policy

Many factors influence judges, e.g.:
- loss allocation (*Nettleship v Weston*);
- protecting professionals (*Hatcher v Black*);
- opening the floodgates.

Judges sometimes refuse to impose a duty on policy grounds, e.g.:
- immunity of judges (*Sirros v Moore*);
- wrongful life (*McKay v Essex A.H.A.*)

2.1 DUTY OF CARE

2.1.1 Negligence – origins and character

1. The modern starting point is Lord Atkin's judgement in *Donoghue v Stevenson* (1932), which established negligence as a separate tort – though its origins were in actions on the case.
2. A new approach was needed, as no other action was available.
3. The judgment contained five key elements.
   - Negligence is a separate tort.
   - Lack of privity of contract is irrelevant to mounting an action.
   - Negligence is proved as a result of satisfying a three-part test:
     (i) there must be a duty of care owed by defendant to claimant;
     (ii) the duty is breached by the defendant falling below the appropriate standard of care;
     (iii) the defendant causes damage to the claimant that is not too remote a consequence of the breach.
   - Lord Atkin's 'Neighbour Principle': 'You must take reasonable care to avoid acts or omissions which you can reasonably foresee would be likely to injure your neighbour. Who, then, in law, is my neighbour? Persons who are so closely and directly affected by my act that I ought reasonably to have them in my contemplation as being affected so when I am directing my mind to the acts or omissions in question'.
   - A manufacturer owes a duty to consumers and users of his products not to cause them harm.
4. Thus broad principles were established to determine liability
5. The law developed incrementally, establishing new duties.
6. Policy has always been a crucial element so the court will not only decide whether there is a duty, but whether there should be.
7. Many factors influence the judges:
   - loss allocation (*Nettleship v Weston* (1971));

- moral considerations;
- practical considerations;
- protecting professionals (*Hatcher v Black* (1954));
- constitutional obligations;
- the 'floodgates' argument;
- the possible benefits of imposing duties (*Smolden v Whitworth and Nolan* (1997)).

8. Judges have often cited policy when refusing a duty of care:
- liability of lawyers (*Rondel v Worsley* (1969)) – but now see *Arthur J S Hall & Co. v Simons & others* (2000);
- liability of police (*Hill v Chief Constable of West Yorkshire* (1988));
- immunity of judges (*Sirros v Moore* (1975));
- alternative ways to compensate, e.g. CICB, MIB;
- rescues (*Salmon v Seafarer Restaurants* (1983));
- specific claims (wrongful life) (*McKay v Essex A.H.A.* (1982));
- where claimant belongs to an indeterminately large group (*Monroe v London Fire and Civil Defence Authority* (1991));
- where claimant is responsible for own misfortune (*Governors of the Peabody Donation Fund v Parkinson* (1984)).

9. At one point Lord Atkin's test was simplified by Lord Wilberforce in *Anns v Merton L.B.C.* (1978) into a two-part test.
   a) Is there sufficient proximity between defendant and claimant to impose a *prima facie* duty?
   b) If so, does the judge consider that there are any policy grounds which would prevent such a duty being imposed?

10. The *Anns* test was always seen as too broad because:
   a) it creates a general duty based only on proximity;
   b) it gives judges too much power to decide on policy alone.

11. A long line of cases expressed dissatisfaction with the Anns test, e.g. (*Governors of Peabody Donation Fund v Sir Lindsay Parkinson* (1985)); (*Caparo v Dickman* (1990). The test was finally overruled in *Murphy v Brentwood D.C.* (1990).

12. It was replaced by a three-part test of Lords Oliver, Keith, Bridge in *Caparo* (1932).
    a) Reasonable foresight (*Fardon v Harcourt-Rivington*) and (*Topp v London Country Bus (South West) Ltd* (1993)), but see also (*Margereson v J.W. Roberts Ltd, Hancock v J.W. Roberts Ltd* (1996)) compared to the earlier rule in (*Gunn v Wallsend Slipway & Engineering Co Ltd* (1989)).
    b) Proximity (*Hill* (1988)) and (*John Munroe v London Fire and Civil Defence Authority* (1997)).
    c) Is it fair and reasonable to impose duty? (*Hemmens v Wilson Browne* (1993)) and (*Ephraim v Newham L.B.C.* (1993)).

13. Subsequent cases have approved this 'incremental' approach (*Spring v Guardian Assurance* (1995)); (*Jones v Wright* (1994)).

14. Policy has inevitably remained a major factor (*Hill* (1988)):
    a) as with public, regulatory bodies compare (*Philcox v Civil Aviation Authority* (1995)) and (*Perrett v Collins* (1998));
    b) and immunity from suit for professionals (*Kelley v Corston* (1997)) and (*Griffin v Kingsmill* (1998));
    c) and also for public services (*Capital & Counties plc v Hampshire County Council* (1997)).

15. The *Anns* test was flawed, but the new test is arguably no better:
    ● it claims to follow the separation of powers theory;
    ● but it is more complex and secret, and restricts development.

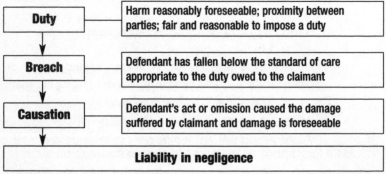

What must be proved for negligence

2.1.2 The duty of care

1. Case law is crucial to identifying duty situations.
2. Negligence is not mere carelessness, so no duty no liability.
3. There must be a 'duty on the facts', not a mere notional duty.
4. The key questions are:
   a) Is the situation or loss of a type to which negligence applies?
   b) Does the defendant owe a duty to the actual claimant?
5. Numerous straightforward situations, e.g. employers/ employees; fellow motorists; doctors/patients, manufacturers/ consumers, etc.
6. However, courts have also considered many controversial situations.

2.2. BREACH OF THE DUTY OF CARE

2.2.1 The Standard of Care and Reasonable Man Test

1. A breach occurs whenever a defendant falls below the standard of care appropriate to the particular duty owed.
2. The standard is objectively measured by the 'reasonable man' test: 'the omission to do something which a reasonable man would do, or doing something which a prudent and reasonable man would not do.' Per Alderson B in *Blyth v Birmingham Waterworks* (1865).
3. The reasonable man has been described as 'the "man on the street" or "the man on the Clapham omnibus" ...'
4. Or, as MacMillan L.J. put it in *Glasgow Corporation v Muir* (1943), the test is 'independent of the idiosyncrasies of the particular person whose conduct is in question ...The reasonable man is presumed to be free from both over-apprehension and over-confidence'.
5. So breach of duty then is merely the same as fault.

The reasonable man test

- A breach occurs when the defendant falls below the standard of care appropriate to the duty owed.
- So breach is doing something which a reasonable, prudent man would not do, or omitting to do something that he would do.
- The reasonable man is said to be free from both over-apprehension and over-confidence.

BREACH OF DUTY

Res ipsa loquitur

Plea reversing burden when negligence impossible to prove. Three ingredients:
- at all material times thing causing damage is in defendant's control (*Gee v Metropolitan Railway*);
- no alternative explanation other than negligence (*Barkway v South Wales Transport*);
- accident of a type usually only caused by negligence (*Scott v London & St Katherine's Docks*).

Factors in determining the standard of care

- Foreseeability (*Roe v Minister of Health*).
- Magnitude of risk (compare *Bolton v Stone* and (*Hale v London Electricity Board*).
- Social utility (*Watt v Hertfordshire CC*).
- Practicality of precautions (*Latimer v AEC*).
- Common practice (*Brown v Rolls Royce*).
- Children (same standard as adults (*Morales v Ecclestone*).
- Motorists (standard of learners is same as for experienced drivers (*Nettleship v Weston*).
- Sport (standard is the standard of reasonable competitors (*Condon v Basi*) or reasonable officials (*Smoldon v Whitworth*).
- Experts or professionals (standard is measured against a reasonable competent body of professional opinion (*Bolam v Friern Hospital Management Committee*).
  (i) Applicable also to professional advice (*Sidaway v Governors of Bethlem Royal & Maudsley Hospitals*).
  (ii) Some practices are unacceptable even if common (*Re Herald of Free Enterprise*).
  (iii) Standard for trainees is the same as for experienced professionals (*Wilsher v Essex Area Health Authority*).
  (iv) But a judge may disregard professional opinion if it is not sustained by logic (*Bolitho v City and Hackney Health Authority*).

6. Factors of policy and expediency are taken into account, e.g.:
- who can best bear the loss;
- whether or not the defendant is insured;
- how the decision might affect future behaviour;
- the justice of the individual case;
- how the decision affects society as a whole.

7. Judges have established criteria by which to measure the standard.

2.2.2 Principles in determining the standard of care

1. Foreseeability: no obligation for defendant to compensate for incidents beyond his normal contemplation or outside his existing knowledge compare (*Roe v Minister of Health* (1954)) with (*Walker v Northumberland County Council* (1995)).

2. Magnitude of risk: the care expected depends on likelihood of risk – compare (*Bolton v Stone* (1951)) with (*Hale v London Electricity Board* (1965)).

3. Social utility: a risk averting a worse danger may be justified (*Watts v Hertfordshire C.C.* (1954)), but not any risk at all (*Griffin v Mersey Regional Ambulance* (1998)).

4. Practicality of precautions: need not take extraordinary steps or suffer extraordinary cost (*Latimer v A.E.C.* (1953)).

5. Common practice: usually, but not always, suggests non-negligent practice (*Brown v Rolls Royce* (1966)).

6. Specific classes of people have specific rules.

   a) **Children**: originally not expected to take same care as adults (*McHale v Watson* (1966)), but see now (*Morales v Ecclestone* (1991) and *Armstrong v Cottrell* (1993)).

   b) **The disabled and sick**: standard appropriate to disability.

   c) **Motorists**: the same standard applies to all drivers, even learners (*Nettleship v Weston* (1971)) and one becoming ill while driving (*Roberts v Ramsbottom* (1980)), but not if unaware of the illness (*Mansfield v Weetabix Ltd* (1997)).

d) **People lacking specialist skills**: not expected to show same standard as a skilled person (*Phillips v Whiteley Ltd* (1938)).

e) **Sport**: standards applicable to reasonable competitors (*Condon v Basi* (1985)), or reasonable officials (*Smoldon v Whitworth* (1997)).

7. **Experts and professionals** are not bound by the standards of a reasonable man but those of a reasonable practitioner of that particular skill or profession (*Bolam v Friern Hospital Management Committee* (1957)).

a) The test also applies to advice and information (*Sidaway v Governors of Bethlem Royal & Maudsley Hospitals* (1985)).

b) So professionals need only provide expert witnesses who agree with conduct in question (*Whitehouse v Jordan* (1981)).

c) Some practices are unacceptable even though common (*Re Herald of Free Enterprise* (1989)).

d) Trainees must show the same degree of skill as experienced professionals (*Wilsher v Essex A.H.A.* (1988)).

e) The test applies even if the defendant does not have full professional qualifications (*Adams v Rhymney Valley D.C.* (2000)).

f) The rule has been approved since 'There is seldom any one answer exclusive of all others to problems of professional judgement. A court may prefer one body of opinion to the other; but that is no basis for a conclusion of negligence ...' Per Lord Scarman in (*Maynard v West Midlands RHA* (1985)).

g) Only a small number of doctors following the practice is sufficient to relieve liability (*De Freitas v O'Brien and Conolly* (1995)), where 11 out of 1000 would have operated.

h) However, the test has been subject to many criticisms:
- it overprotects professionals;
- it allows the professionals to set the standard;
- it is inconsistent with negligence principles generally;
- it can often legitimize quite marginal practices;
- definition of a competent body of opinion is too imprecise;
- the test can lead to professionals closing ranks.

i) Numerous recent cases have challenged its authority:
- (*Newell v Goldberg* (1995));
- (*Lybert v Warrington HA* (1996));
- (*Thompson v James and Others* (1996)) – failure by GP to follow guidelines in warnings about measles vaccinations, and claimant brain damaged as a result.

j) If the judge feels that the opinion held is not sustained by logic, then it may be disregarded (*Bolitho v City and Hackney Health Authority* (1997)).

2.2.3 Proof of negligence and res ipsa loquitur

1. Normally the burden of proof is on the claimant, who has the hard task of collecting evidence.
2. This can be relaxed in two instances:
   a) for criminal convictions under s11 Civil Evidence Act 1968;
   b) if the plea of *res ipsa loquitur* is raised.
3. Literally translated this means 'the thing speaks for itself'.
4. Succeeding with the plea means burden of proof is reversed.
5. However, (*Wilsher* (1987)) suggests that it merely raises a refutable presumption of negligence.
6. It is narrowly construed for fairness – the facts must conform to the criteria in (*Scott v London & St Katherine Docks* (1865)).

7. There are three essential requirements for the plea to succeed.
   a) At all material times the thing causing injury or damage must have been in defendant's control. Compare *Gee v Metropolitan Railway Co.* (1873) with *Easson v London and North Eastern Railway* (1944).
   b) The incident has no obvious alternative explanation (*Barkway v South Wales Transport Co. Ltd* (1950)).
   c) The accident is of a type which would not occur if proper care was shown so is of a type commonly caused by negligence (*Scott v London & St Katherine's Docks* (1865)); (*Mahon v Osborne* (1939)); and (*Ward v Tesco Stores* (1976)).
8. It is debatable whether *res ipsa* applies in medical negligence but it is often pleaded because of a difficulty in gaining evidence.
9. However, it has been rejected by both the courts and Pearson because of fear of escalating claims and insurance premiums.

2.2.4 Strict liability in negligence

1. *Res ipsa loquitur* formerly applied to foreign bodies in food.
2. Consumer Protection Act (1987) was introduced to comply with EU directives.
   - It introduced strict liability on anyone in the distribution chain where the consumer suffers harm.
   - Fault liability was removed, but causation is still required.

Causation in fact
Based on 'but for' test (if harm would not have occurred but for defendant's act/omission, the defendant liable (*Barnett v Chelsea & Kensington Hospital Management Committee*).
If there are multiple causes:
● Defendant may not be liable for all of damage if claimant has pre-existing condition (*Cutler v Vauxhall Motors*);
● multiple concurrent causes may defeat claim (*Wilsher v Essex AHA*);
● with consecutive causes there is no liability for second event unless it causes extra damage (*Performance Cars v Abraham*), but see (*Baker v Willoughby*) and (*Jobling v Associated Dairies*) on under or over compensating the claimant.

CAUSATION

Novus actus interveniens
A new act intervenes and relieves defendant of liability (can be act of:
● claimant (*McKew v Holland & Hannon & Cubitts*);
● nature (*Carslogie Steamship Co v Royal Norwegian Government*);
● third party – compare (*Knightley v Johns* and *Rouse v Squires*).

Remoteness of damage
● For claimant to recover, damage must not be too remote a consequence of the breach.
● Originally measured on direct consequence (*Re Polemis*).
● Now measured on foreseeability (*The Wagon Mound*).
● Only the general type of harm need be foreseen, not the actual extent (*Bradford v Robinson Rentals*).
● The 'thin skull rule' applies – defendant must take claimant as he finds him (*Paris v Stepney BC*).

2.3 CAUSATION AND REMOTENESS OF DAMAGE

2.3.1 Introduction

1. Once duty and breach are shown it must also be proved that the defendant's act or omission caused the damage.
2. Claimant must prove causal link on a balance of probabilities.
3. This may be difficult if there are multiple causes or the type of damage is unusual.
4. Policy considerations are still crucial to causation.
5. Must show: defendant's act or omission caused loss or injury to claimant (causation in fact); and sufficient proximity between act and damage to fix defendant with liability (causation in law).

2.3.2 Causation in fact

1. Based on 'but for' test – Lord Denning in *Cork v Kirby Maclean Ltd* (1952): 'if the damage would not have happened but for a particular fault, then that fault is the cause of the damage; if it would have happened just the same, fault or no fault, the fault is not the cause of the damage ...'.
2. Often straightforwardly proved by the facts (*Barnett v Chelsea & Kensington Hospital Management Committee* (1969)).
3. However, problems may exist in proving cause:
   a) it is more about apportioning blame than scientific enquiry;
   b) level of knowledge/scientific advance may make pinpointing exact cause impossible (*Wilsher v Essex AHA* (1988)).
   c) the case law is often contradictory:
      - it may be unfair to the claimant (*Hotson v East Berkshire AHA* (1987)) but see (*Stovold v Barlows* (1995));
      - it may be unfair to the defendant (*McGhee v National Coal Board* (1973));
      - occasionally courts adopt a pragmatic/realistic approach

4. Multiple causes.
   a) Proving a causal link is always difficult if there is more than one cause.
   b) The problem occurs in one of three ways:
      - claimant has pre-existing condition – defendant may not be liable for all damage (*Cutler v Vauxhall Motors* (1971));
      - multiple concurrent causes, but for test will fail here compare (*McGhee v NCB*) and (*Wilsher v Essex AHA*);
      - consecutive causes:
        (i) if second event caused no extra damage liability remains with first event (*Performance Cars v Abraham* (1962));
        (ii) but see *Baker v Willoughby* (1970) and (*Jobling v Associated Dairies* (1982)), which concern neither under or over compensating the claimant.

2.3.3 Novus actus interveniens

1. Translates as 'a new act intervenes', i.e. the chain of causation is broken by a subsequent act the court accepts is the true cause of damage.
2. The effect is to relieve the defendant of liability.
3. It does not apply if the later act is not accepted as the cause of damage (*Kirkham v Chief Constable of Greater Manchester* (1990)).
4. Cases fall into three categories.
   a) An intervening act by claimant – more than contributory negligence since it breaks the chain of causation. Compare (*McKew v Holland & Hannon & Cubitts (Scotland) Ltd* (1969)) with (*Wieland v Cyril Lord Carpets* (1969)).
   b) An intervening act of nature:
      - rarely succeeds because it means claimant has no remedy;
      - defendant may succeed if the natural act is unforeseeable and independent of his own negligence

(*Carslogie Steamship Co. v Royal Norwegian Government* (1952)).

c) intervening act of a third party
  - the act must be sufficient to break the chain of causation;
  - it must be foreseeable;
  - the defendant must not owe a duty to avoid it compare *Knightly v Johns* (1982) with *Rouse v Squires* (1973).

2.3.4 Remoteness of damage

1. Despite proof of a causal link the claimant may fail to recover if damage is said to be too remote a consequence of the breach.

2. It is a legal test based on policy, to avoid overburdening defendant.

3. In the old test the claimant could recover direct consequence loss, even if unforeseeable (*Re Polemis and Furness, Withy & Co* (1921)).

4. The test was criticised for its failure to distinguish between degrees of negligence. Viscount Simmonds in the *Wagon Mound (No 1)* (1961): 'It does not seem consonant with current ideas of justice or morality, that for an act of negligence, however slight, which results in some trivial foreseeable damage, the actor should be liable for all the consequences, however unforeseeable and however grave, so long as they can be said to be direct.'

5. So the test was changed to one of 'reasonable foreseeability' in the *Wagon Mound (No1)* (1961).

6. The type rather than the extent of damage must be foreseen (*Bradford v Robinson Rentals* (1967)) and now (*Margereson v J.W. Roberts Ltd, Hancock v J.W. Roberts* (1996)).

7. Or the precise circumstances must be foreseen (*Hughes v The Lord Advocate* (1963)).

8. There is a broad view of foreseeability to personal injury, except in (*Doughty v Turner Manufacturing* (1964) and *Tremain v Pike* (1969)).

9. But a narrower approach is taken to property damage:
   - so in *Wagon Mound (No1)* the trial judge agreed some damage (fouling) possibly foreseeable, but fire was not, so no liability;
   - but in *Wagon Mound (No2)* the trial judge had suggested that fire was possible but too remote, so Privy Council reversed him.

10. The defendant must take the claimant as he finds him – the so-called 'thin skull rule'.
    - So the defendant is liable for the full extent of damage where the claimant's extra sensitivity caused worse damage (*Paris v Stepney B.C.* (1951)) and (*Smith v Leech Brain Ltd* (1962)).
    - This also applies where likely harm is psychiatric (*Walker v Northumberland County Council* (1994)).
    - It also applies if shock is suffered but no physical injury (*Page v Smith* (1995)).
    - And it applies if the claimant's impecuniosity (lack of means) may be the feature (*Mattocks v Mann* (1993)).

11. The difference between the two tests appears minimal:
    - most reasonably foreseeable consequences are also natural;
    - the thin skull rule means that even many unforeseeable consequences are still liable to compensation;
    - insurance covers many, if not most, types of loss.

2.4 NERVOUS SHOCK

1. This is a complex area which has both expanded and contracted.
2. It must involve an actual psychiatric condition, e.g. post-traumatic stress disorder; Temporary grief or fright is insufficient.
3. Originally cases failed on the 'floodgates' argument and fear of faking (*Victoria Railway Commissioners v Coultas* (1888)).
4. Liability was originally based on the Kennedy test (real and immediate personal danger must be foreseeable (*Dulieu v White* (1901)).

Development of liability

● Originally no action possible because of lack of expertise on psychiatric illness (*Victoria Railway Commissioners v Coultas*).

● Liability first accepted where claimant also at risk of physical injury (*Dulieu v White*).

● Then extended to cover fear for close family when within area of impact (*Hambrook v Stokes*).

● Then to include claimants not within area of impact but within area of shock (*Bourhill v Young*).

● Widest point of liability when claimant not present at scene but present at immediate aftermath and close ties with victim (*McLoughlin v O'Brien*).

NERVOUS SHOCK

Recognised psychiatric illness

● Can be post-traumatic stress disorder or depression.

● Also pathological grief (*Tredget v Bexley HA*).

● But not claustrophobia (*Reilly v Merseyside RHS*).

Criteria for liability

Contained in *Alcock v Chief Constable of West Yorkshire* and distinguishing between primary and secondary victims — claimants can be:

● present at scene and injured (primary) (*Page v Smith*);

● present at scene and at risk of physical harm (primary) (*Dulieu v White*);

● close tie of love and affection with victim and witnessed unaided the incident or its immediate aftermath (secondary) (*McLoughlin v O'Brien*);

● claimant proves a close tie with the victim and witnessed close-ups of the victim on TV in breach of broadcasting rules (secondary).

Professional rescuers have traditionally been accepted as legitimate claimants (*Chadwick v BR Board*). Now they need to be:

● at risk and thus primary victims also to succeed (*White v Chief Constable of West Yorkshire*);

● or a genuine secondary victim (*Greatorex v Greatorex*).

Claimants who will fail include:

● those suffering pre-accident terror (*Hicks v Chief Constable of West Yorkshire*);

● mere bystanders (*McFarlane v E E Caledonia*);

● workmates of victims (*Duncan v British Coal*) and (*Robertson & Rough v Forth Road Bridge*);

● when shock develops gradually (*Sion v Hampstead HA*).

5. The principle was then extended to cover family and close friends (*Hambrook v Stokes* (1925)).

6. It was extended further, to close workmates (*Dooley v Cammel-Laird* (1951)).

7. But it was then limited to claimant being in the area of impact. Compare (*King v Phillips* (1953)) and (*Attia v British Gas* (1987)).

8. Then an alternative was introduced where the claimant was outside the area of impact but within the area of shock. Compare (*Bourhill v Young* (1943)) with (*Ravenscroft v Rederiaktiebolaget* (1991)).

9. There are, in any case, incongruous judgements (*Owens v Liverpool Corp.* (1933)) .

10. The high point of liability came in (*McLoughlin v O'Brien* (1981)) – succeeded even though not a witness of the incident, but this came under Wilberforce's two-part test (there was proximity and no policy reason for denying the claim).

11. Rescuers can claim (*Chadwick v BR Board* (1993)) and (*Hale v London Underground* (1992)), and police at one point succeeded where relatives of Hillsborough victims failed (*Frost v Chief Constable of South Yorkshire* (1996)). Now a rescuer must be a primary victim and at risk to succeed (*White v Chief Constable of South Yorkshire* (1999)), or a genuine secondary victim (*Greatorex v Greatorex* (2000)).

12. Restrictions now exist (*Alcock v Chief Constable of South Yorkshire* (1991)) for secondary victims there are three key requirements to determine. The claimant must:
    - be sufficiently proximate in time and space to the incident;
    - have a close tie of love and affection to the victim;
    - see or hear the incident or its immediate aftermath.

13. *Alcock* (1991) suggests future successful claims will be based on:
    - claimant present at scene and injured (primary victim) (*Page v Smith* (1996));

- claimant present at scene and own safety threatened (primary victim) (*Dulieu v White* (1901));
- claimant proves a close tie with the victim and witnessed the incident or its immediate aftermath at close hand (secondary victim) (*McLoughlin v O'Brien* (1981));
- claimant is a rescuer or one of the professional services (*Piggott v London Underground* (1995)), but see (*Duncan v British Coal* (1996)) and (*White* (1999));
- claimant proves a close tie with the victim and witnessed close-ups of the victim on TV in breach of broadcasting rules;
- claimant shows a close tie with the victim and witnessed the catastrophic event involving victim on TV (more debatable).

14. Claims for pre-accident terror have also been rejected (*Hicks v Chief Constable of South Yorkshire* (1992)).

15. Bystanders have no claim (*McFarlane v E E Caledonia* (1994)).

16. Nor do workmates witnessing the incident without sufficiently close ties (*Robertson and Rough v Forth Road Bridge* (1995)).

17. Nor does it apply where the shock happens gradually rather than suddenly (*Sion v Hampstead HA* (1994)).

18. Many cases now focus on:
    a) the nature of the psychiatric illness:
       - (*Reilly v Merseyside RHA* (1994)) – claustrophobia and subsequent insomnia was insufficient for a claim;
       - (*Tredget v Bexley HA* (1994)) – death of newborn baby did create liability because the trauma created a psychiatric disorder.
    b) causation:
       - (*Calscione v Dixon* (1994)) (no causal link between PTSD and accident;
       - (*Vernon v Bosely* (1996)) (there was a causal link between death of children and pathological grief amounting to a psychiatric disorder.

Original position
- No liability for a pure economic loss, e.g. loss of profit (*Spartan Steels v Martin*).
- Because more appropriate to contract law.

Origins of liability
- Some liability in (*Dutton v Bognor Regis UDC*) because of risk to health.
- Developed in (*Anns v Merton LBC*) as a result of Lord Wilberforce's two-part test – proximity and policy.
- Developed further in (*Junior Books v Veitchi*) because claimant nominated sub-contractors (so no action in contract); defendant knew claimants relied on their skill; damage was direct and foreseeable consequence of their breach.

PURE ECONOMIC LOSS

Modern position
- Many cases expressed dissatisfaction with (*Anns*, e.g. *D & F Estates v Church Commissioners*).
- So two-part test overruled in (*Murphy v Brentwood*).
- Artificial divide between property damage and pure economic loss discredited in (*Marc Rich v Bishop Rock Marine*)
- Current policy favours private insurance.

2.5 PURE ECONOMIC LOSS

1. The courts have always been reluctant to accept claims for pure economic loss, since it is more closely linked to contract law.
2. However, they have kept a distinction between economic loss caused by negligent statements and that caused by negligent acts.
   - The distinction was originally seen as mainly one of policy (*Spartan Steels v Martin & Co. (contractors) Ltd* (1973)).
   - The purpose being to limit any extension of liability.
3. It was confirmed in (*Weller v Foot & Mouth Research Institute* (1966)); (*Meah v Creamer* (1986)); (*Pritchard v Cobden* (1988)).
4. Liability was extended in (*Dutton v Bognor Regis U.D.C.* (1972)).

- Although it was not clear-cut whether this was under *Hedley Byrne* or *Donoghue*.
- The justification for liability was risk to health.

5. Liability was expanded:
   - as a result of the two-part test in (*Anns v Merton L.B.C.* (1978));
   - and also for a possible future threat to health (*Batty v Metropolitan Property Realisations* (1978)).

6. The 'high water mark' was (*Junior Books v Veitchi Co. Ltd* (1983)).
   a) There were three key issues:
      - claimant nominated defendants to lay their floor in the new printing works, so relied on their skill;
      - defendant knew of this reliance by the claimant;
      - damage was a direct and foreseeable consequence of the defendant's negligence.
   b) Lord Brandon dissented because the case extended tortious liability into contract areas.

7. Many later cases expressed dissatisfaction with *Junior Books*:
   - (*Governors of the Peabody Donation Fund v Sir Lindsay Parkinson* (1984));
   - (*Muirhead v Industrial Tank Specialists Ltd* (1985));
   - (*D & F Estates v Church Commissioners* (1988));
   - (*Reid v Ruth* (1989)).

8. The *Anns* two-part test was overruled in (*Murphy v Brentwood D.C.* (1990)).

9. This was followed in (*Department. of the Environment v Thomas Bates & Sons Ltd* (1990)).

10. The artificial divide between damage to property and pure economic loss has been further discredited in (*Marc Rich & Co. v Bishop Rock Marine* (1995)).

11. So the present policy favours private insurance rather than tort.

12. However, judges have shown themselves willing to be more relaxed in response to specific policy considerations (*Spring v Guardian Assurance* (1994)) involving negligent references.

2.6 NEGLIGENT MISSTATEMENT

2.6.1 The origins of liability

1. Tort remedies physical loss and damage, but judges are reluctant to allow recovery for a pure economic loss since it is considered to be more appropriate to contract law.
2. Successful actions originally involved misrepresentations made fraudulently, not those made negligently.
3. Any action would be in the tort of deceit (*Derry v Peek* (1889)).
4. Principle reaffirmed in (*Candler v Crane Christmas & Co* (1951)).
5. But the impetus for creating liability came from Lord Denning's dissenting judgement in this case: defendants should owe a duty of care to 'any third person to whom they themselves show the accounts, or to whom they know their employer is going to show the accounts so as to induce them to invest money or take some other action upon them ...'.
6. Lord Denning's judgement was finally approved *in obiter* in (*Hedley Byrne v Heller & Partners Ltd* (1964)).
   a) While the action failed because a valid disclaimer was used, HL accepted a duty of care might exist despite:
      • the absence of a contractual relationship;
      • the fact that it would mean imposing liability for economic loss.
   b) HL also laid down criteria for allowing such liability:
      • existence of a special relationship between the parties;
      • special skill possessed by person giving advice;
      • presence of reasonable reliance on the advice.
   c) The basic principles have since been accepted and developed in case law.

Origins of liability
- Originally courts hostile to accepting liability for any economic loss, since more appropriate to contract law.
- Same reasoning applied in relation to negligently prepared accounts in (*Candler v Crane Christmas & Co*).
- Lord Denning, dissenting, thought there should be liability for negligent preparation of accounts to third parties as well as the client.
- Reasoning accept in (*Hedley Byrne v Heller & Partners*) where HL suggested for liability:
  i) there must be a special relationship;
  ii) person giving advice must have specialist skill of kind needed for advice;
  iii) must be reliance on the advice.

Criteria for imposing duty
Special relationship
- Generally means where person is expected to give advice.
- Has been suggested could include business arrangements (*Howard Marine & Dredging v Ogden & Sons*).
- But generally not social relationships (*Chaudhry v Prabhakar*).
- Can involve surveyors (*Yianni v Edwin Evans*).
- But the position on accountants is less clear-cut (*Caparo v Dickman*).

Possession of special skills
- Duty only exists if defendant has skill in area of advice given (*Mutual Life & Citizens Assurance v Evatt*).
- So no liability for uninformed advice (*Chaudhry v Prabhaker*).

Reasonable reliance on the advice
- No liability unless statement affected claimant's judgment (*JEB Fasteners v Mark Bloom*).
- Policy can affect outcome, e.g. no liability if advisee a member of too large a class (*Goodwill v British Pregnancy Advisory Service*).
- Defendant must know claimant would rely on advice (*Yianni v Edwin Evans*).
- Such knowledge can even invalidate exclusion clauses (*Harris v Wyre Forest DC & Smith v Eric S Bush*).

NEGLIGENT MISSTATEMENT

Inconsistent cases
- Person receiving advice was not loss sufferer (*Ross v Caunters*).
- Foreseeability of reliance creates liability (*Ministry of Housing and Local Government v Sharp*).
- Policy dictates liability and ensures a remedy (*White v Jones*).

Current state of the law
HL have since expanded on where a duty will apply in *Caparo v Dickman*.
- advice is required for purpose either specified in detail or described in general terms to defendant;
- purpose is made known, actually or by inference, to advisor at the time advice is given;
- advisor knows, actually or inferentially, that advice will be communicated to person relying on it to use for known purpose, and that advice will be acted upon without further independent advice;
- person relying on advice acts on it to their detriment.

2.6.2 The criteria for imposing liability

The special relationship

1. The meaning of 'special relationship' was not fully explained in *Hedley Byrne*, so has become an area for judicial policy.
2. Originally a narrow interpretation was preferred, to include only a relationship where the person was expected to give advice of the kind given.
3. It has later been suggested that any business or professional relationship has potential to be special relationship (*Howard Marine & Dredging Co. Ltd v Ogden & Sons Ltd* (1978)).
4. It is not possible in a purely social relationship unless circumstances show that carefully considered advice was being sought (*Chaudhry v Prabhaker* (1988)).
5. Many cases involve surveyors or valuers. The relationship between surveyors and purchasers of houses might be special although not contractual (*Yianni v Edwin Evans & Sons* (1982)).
6. One complex issue is to whom accountants owe a duty of care:
   a) it has influenced how the existence of the duty is determined;
   b) originally there was held to be no duty, since any duty would be contractual (*Candler v Crane Christmas & Co* (1951));
   c) since *Hedley Byrne* the existence of the duty has been established (*JEB Fasteners v Marks Bloom & Co.* (1983));
   d) bidders in a take-over or lenders or investors of any kind cannot rely on the annual audited accounts, so there is no duty on the accountants (*Caparo v Dickman* (1990)).

The possession of special skill

1. Duty only exists if defendant possesses skill in area of advice given (*Mutual Life & Citizens Assurance Co. v Evatt* (1971)).
2. So there is usually no liability usually for advice of an uninformed and inexpert character but see (*Chaudhry v Prabhaker* (1988)).

Reasonable reliance on the advice

1. If a negligent statement did not influence the claimant's judgement then no liability (*JEB Fasteners v Marks Bloom & Co. Ltd* (1983)) and (*Lambert v West Devon Borough Council* (1997)).

2. As with special relationship, reasonable reliance has been a subject for judicial policy (*Caparo v Dickman* (1990)).

   a) So reliance is not automatic in a relationship of trust (*Jones v Wright* (1994)).

   b) Neither is there reliance if the claimant belongs to too large a group (*Goodwill v British Pregnancy Advisory Service* (1996)).

3. The defendant must have known or be reasonably expected to have known that the claimant would rely upon the advice (*Yianni v Edwin Evans* (1982)).

4. Foreseeability of reliance can even invalidate exclusions (*Harris v Wyre Forest D.C.* (1989)) and (*Smith v Eric S Bush* (1990)).

5. A disclaimer may be declared unreasonable and invalid, but a surveyor can still use one to discharge his duty and avoid liability (*Eley v Chasemore* (1989)).

2.6.3 The current state of the law

1. The property and financial markets boom of the late 1980s led to a large number of cases involving surveyors or accountants.

2. In (*Caparo v Dickman* (1990), HL restated principles involved for both special relationships and reasonable reliance.

   a) HL preferred an incremental approach to duty of care.

   b) HL rejected a general test based on reasonable foresight, and led to a later request for leave to amend the statement of claim in (*Morgan Crucible plc v Hill Samuel Bank Ltd* (1991)).

   c) HL explained that a duty will apply where:

      ● the advice is required for a purpose, either specified in detail or described in general times to the defendant;

> ● the purpose is made known, actually or by inference, to the advisor at the time the advice is given;
> ● the advisor knows, actually or inferentially, that the advice will be communicated to the person relying on it to use for the known purpose;
> ● the advice will be acted upon without further independent advice;
> > ● the person relying on the advice acts on it to their detriment.

3. This is a narrow approach, reflecting the move away from *Anns*. Later cases have given further advice on when a duty exists. CA in (*James Mcnaughten Papers Group Ltd v Hicks Anderson & Co.* (1991)) identified areas for consideration:
   a) the purpose for which the statement was made;
   b) the purpose ofcommunicating the statement;
   c) the relationship between the advisor, the recipient of the advice and any third parties;
   d) the size of the class to which the recipient belongs;
   e) the knowledge and experience possessed by the advisee;
   f) whether it was reasonable to rely on the advice.

4. Significantly, however, the narrowing in *Caparo* is at odds with EU law, which requires harmonization of company law, including the principle that a company's auditors owe a duty of care to third parties who suffer financial loss as a result of negligence.

5. Subsequent cases suggest some relaxation of the law (*Henderson v Merrett Syndicates Ltd* (1994)); (*Aiken v Steward Wrightson Members Agency Ltd* (1995)); (*N M Rothschild and Sons Ltd v Berensons and Others* (1995)).

2.6.4 Cases inconsistent with the general principle

1. Some cases do not conform because the person relying on the advice is not the one suffering loss (*Ross v Caunters* (1980)).

2. Liability occurs because it is reasonably foreseeable that the party relies on the advice, and indeed that such a party exists (*Ministry of Housing & Local Government v Sharp* (1971)).

3. Following *Henderson* there may still not be liability if there is no assumption of responsibility, or if the evidence shows the contrary (*McCullagh v Lane Fox and Partners* (1995)).

4. Policy determines liability in such cases to prevent a party being unreasonably denied any remedy (*White v Jones* (1995)) and (*Gorham v British Telecommunications Plc* (2000).

5. Debatable whether duty exists under Donoghue v Stevenson principles (*Spring v Guardian Assurance Plc* (1994)).

2.7 OMISSIONS

1. The general rule is for no liability for omissions (non-feasance).

2. The reasons are fairly obvious:
   - causation is significantly harder, if not impossible, to prove;
   - it imposes too onerous an obligation on the defendant.

3. Exceptions have developed that Lord Goff has listed in (*Smith v Littlewoods Organisation Ltd* (1987)).

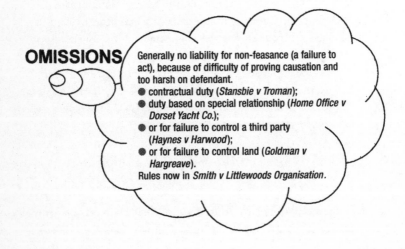

OMISSIONS

Generally no liability for non-feasance (a failure to act), because of difficulty of proving causation and too harsh on defendant.
- contractual duty (*Stansbie v Troman*);
- duty based on special relationship (*Home Office v Dorset Yacht Co.*);
- or for failure to control a third party (*Haynes v Harwood*);
- or for failure to control land (*Goldman v Hargreave*).

Rules now in *Smith v Littlewoods Organisation*.

- A contractual or other undertaking: (*Barnet v Chelsea & Kensington Hospital Management Committee* (1969)); (*Mercer v SE & Chatham Railway* (1922)); (*Stansbie v Troman* (1948)); but see (*Hill v Chief Constable of W. Yorkshire* (1998)).
- A special relationship between the defendant and a third party (*Home Office v Dorset Yacht Co.* (1976)) and (*Barrett v Ministry of Defence* (1993)), but there is a possibility of *volenti* (*Selfe v Ilford District Hospital Management Committee* (1970)).
- A failure to exercise control over a third party (*Haynes v Harwood* (1935)).
- A failure to control land or dangerous things. Compare *Cunningham v Reading F.C.* (1978)) with (*Goldman v Hargreave* (1966)).

CHAPTER 3

OCCUPIER'S LIABILITY

Parties to action
● **Defendants:**
occupiers are those in control of premises at material time (*Wheat v Lacon*).
● **Claimants 1957 Act:**
visitors includes: inviteees, licensees, people entering under a contract, people with a legal right to enter.
● **Claimants 1984 Act:**
non-visitors include: trespassers, people using private rights of way (*Holden v Wright*), people entering under National Parks and Access to Countryside Act.
● **Claimants common law:**
those using public rights of way.

Scope of duty in 1957 Act
● **Common duty of care:**
by s2(1) occupier owes same duty to all visitors.
● **Standard of care:**
by s2(2) occupier must take reasonable steps to ensure visitor safe for legitimate purpose of visit.
● **Avoiding the duty:**
   i) warnings are acceptable if effective to keep the visitor safe (*Rae v Mars*);
   ii) excursions are possible by agreement or otherwise, but not, e.g. for sub-contractors, or those with legal right to enter;
   iii) contributory negligence can reduce damages (*Sayers v Harlow UDC*);
   iv) *volenti* is possible if risk is genuinely accepted (*White v Blackmore*).

OCCUPIER'S LIABILITY

Liability under 1984 Act
● Based on common duty of humanity (*Herrington v B R Board*).
● Available for personal injury only.
● Under s1(3) duty if: aware of danger, and knows or believes the non-visitor is in danger, and risk is one occupier should guard against.

Special cases
Children:
● by s2(3) premises must be safe for child of age;
● there should be no allurements (*Glasgow Corporation v Taylor*);
● occupier can expect parents to care for young children (*Phipps v Rochester Corporation*).
Those exercising a trade:
● by s2(3) must guard against risks associated with their trade (*Roles v Nathan*).
● but occupier can still be liable (*Salmon v Seafarers Restaurant*).
Liability for acts of independent contractors:
no liability if reasonable to hire out work, competent contractor chosen, and work inspected if necessary (*Haseldine v Daw*).

3.1 LIABILITY TO LAWFUL VISITORS UNDER THE 1957 ACT

3.1.1 Introduction

1. Occupier's Liability Act 1957 – covers liability to visitors.
2. 1984 Act covers liability to non-visitors (mainly trespassers).
3. Both Acts only cover damage resulting from state of premises – other damage is covered by negligence (*Ogwo v Taylor* (1987)).

3.1.2 Definition of occupier (potential defendants

1. There is no real statutory definition so common law test applies: who has control of premises (*Wheat v Lacon* (1966)).
2. Dual occupation possible – identity of the defendant depends on the nature of the interest, etc. (*Collier v Anglian Water Authority* (1983)).
3. In an action a lawyer's main concern is who has means to be sued.
4. There is no need for proprietary interest or possession, only control, so different to trespass (*Harris v Birkenhead Corporation* (1976)).

3.1.3 Definition of premises

1. No complete definition in either Act, so common law applies.
2. It obviously includes houses, buildings, land, etc. but also:
- ships in dry dock (*London Graving Dock v Horton* (1951));
- vehicles (*Hartwell v Grayson* (1947));
- lifts (*Haseldine v Daw & Son Ltd* (1941));
- aircraft (*Fosbroke-Hobbes v Airwork Ltd* (1937));
- and even a ladder (*Wheeler v Copas* (1981)).
3. The 1957 Act in s1(3)(a) preserves the common law ('fixed or movable structure, including any vessel, vehicle or aircraft ...'.

3.1.4 Potential claimants

1. The 1957 Act simplified complex common law classes of
   entrant. These were:
   - invitee – enters in material interest of occupier, e.g. a shop
     customer, a friend visiting;
   - licensee – mere permission, e.g. a person taking a short cut;
   - a person entering under a contract, e.g. a painter (duty
     depended on contract) – a sub-contractor is only a licensee;
   - a person entering by legal right, e.g. meter readers, police
     executing warrants, but also private and public rights of
     way;
   - trespassers – no permission and no rights.
2. The different classes were owed different duties so s1(2) 1957
   Act was replaced with 'common duty of care' to 'visitors',
   including:
   - licensees and invitees – implied licensees must show license
     created by occupier's conduct (*Lowery v Walker* (1911));
   - those entering under a contract – where the contract
     provides for greater protection it will be owed;
   - those entering by legal right.
3. Visitor does not include:
   - private rights of way (*Holden v Wright* (1982));
   - those entering under an access agreement under the
     National Parks & Access to Countryside Act;
   - trespassers (all covered by Occupiers Liability Act 1984);
   - public rights of way, covered by the common law
     (*McGeown v Northern Ireland Housing Executive* (1994)).

3.1.5 The scope of the Act (the common duty of care

1. By s2(1), 'An Occupier of premises owes the same duty, the
   common duty of care to all his visitors except insofar as he is
   free to do and does extend, restrict, modify or exclude his duty.'
2. By s2(2) duty is to 'take such care as in all circumstances ... is
   reasonable to see that the visitor will be reasonably safe in

using the premises for the purpose for which he is invited ...'.
3. Three key points apply.
   a) The standard of care is the same as for negligence – no need to guard against the unforeseeable (*Bolton v Stone* (1951)).
   b) Duty only exists while the visitor carries out authorised activities.
   c) The visitor must be kept safe, not the premises, so the Act elaborates on certain classes of visitor.

3.1.6 Liability to children

1. S2(3) allows for 'children to be less careful than adults' and 'premises must be reasonably safe for a child of that age ...'.
2. So the standard of care owed to a child is measured subjectively
3. This is because an unthreatening object to an adult may be dangerous to a child (*Moloney v Lambeth LBC* (1966)).
4. Occupiers must not lead children into temptation (the 'allurement principle' (*Glasgow Corporation v Taylor* (1922)).
5. However, allurement is not definite proof of liability (*Liddle v Yorkshire (North Riding) CC* (1944)).
6. It had been held that there is no liability where there is an allurement but the type of damage sustained is not foreseeable (*Jolley v London Borough of Sutton* (1998)) CA, but HL (2000) subsequently held that if damage is foreseeable then there is liability even if the way in which it is caused is not foreseeable.
7. Parents may be expected to be responsible for very young children (*Phipps v Rochester Corporation* (1955)).

3.1.7 Liability to persons entering to exercise a calling

1. By s2(3)(b) a person carrying out a trade 'will appreciate and guard against any special risks ordinarily incident to it ...'.

2. So tradesmen are expected to avoid the risks associated with their trade (*Roles v Nathan* (1963)).
3. An employer may still be liable for failing to provide safe systems of work (*General Cleaning Contractors v Christmas* (1953)).
4. The fact the visitor has a skilled calling is not proof *per se* of the occupier's liability (*Salmon v Seafarer Restaurants Ltd* (1983)).

3.1.8 Liability for the acts of independent contractors

Under s2(4) there is no liability for 'faulty execution of any work or construction, maintenance or repair by an independent contractor ...' providing:

a) it was reasonable to entrust the work – compare *Haseldine v Daw* with *Woodward v Mayor of Hastings* (1945);
b) a competent contractor was hired (*Ferguson v Welsh* (1987));
c) if necessary the occupier checked work was carried out properly (*AMF International Ltd v Magnet Bowling Ltd* (1968)).

3.1.9 Avoiding the duty

1. Warnings
a) By s2(4) warning relieves liability if 'in all circumstances it was enough to enable the visitor to be reasonably safe.'
b) What is sufficient warning is a question of fact in each case.
c) A warning may be insufficient and a barrier be necessary instead (*Rae v Mars (UK) Ltd* (1990)).
d) Genuine warnings, e.g. 'Danger steps slippery when wet' must be distinguished from attempts to use the defence of *volenti*, e.g. 'Persons enter at their own risk', and

exclusions, e.g. 'No liability accepted for accidents, however caused.'

e) If the danger is obvious to all the occupier can assume that the visitor will take care (*Staples v West Dorset D.C.* (1995)).

2. Exclusions:

a) Under s2(1) exclusions are allowed 'by agreement or otherwise ...', so can exclude by a term of the contract or by a communicating notice (*Ashdown v Samuel Williams* (1957)).

b) Restrictions on the principle include:

- excluding liability to persons entering by a legal right is not possible;
- nor is excluding liability when bound by a contract to admit strangers to a contract (sub-contractors);
- the Occupier's Liability Act 1957 imposes minimum standard, so one argument is that excluding liability standard should not be possible or trespassers will have greater rights than lawful visitors;
- exclusions may well fail against children;
- s1(3) of UCTA applies in business premises.

3. Defences

a) Contributory negligence under The Law Reform (Contributory Negligence) Act 1945 when appropriate.

b) *Volenti non fit injuria* (s2(5) allows that there is no liability for risks willingly undertaken:

- if risk is fully understood (*Simms v Leigh RFC* (1960));
- mere knowledge of a risk is insufficient to raise defence – must have accepted it (*White v Blackmore* (1972));
- where claimant has no choice then there is no consent (*Burnett v British Waterways* (1973));
- express warnings of claimant entering at own risk are probably caught by UCTA.

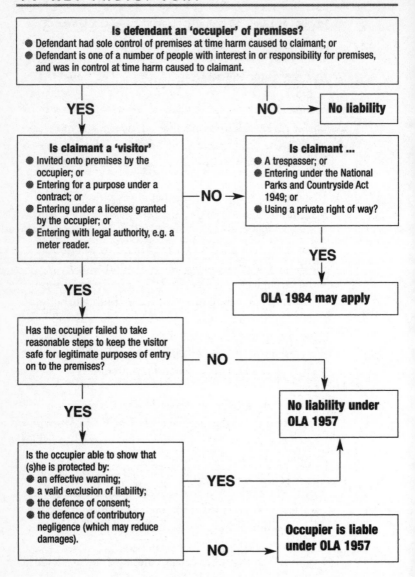

Is defendant an 'occupier' of premises?
- Defendant had sole control of premises at time harm caused to claimant; or
- Defendant is one of a number of people with interest in or responsibility for premises, and was in control at time harm caused to claimant.

YES

NO → No liability

Is claimant a 'visitor'
- Invited onto premises by the occupier; or
- Entering for a purpose under a contract; or
- Entering under a license granted by the occupier; or
- Entering with legal authority, e.g. a meter reader.

NO →

Is claimant ...
- A trespasser; or
- Entering under the National Parks and Countryside Act 1949; or
- Using a private right of way?

YES

OLA 1984 may apply

YES

Has the occupier failed to take reasonable steps to keep the visitor safe for legitimate purposes of entry on to the premises?

— NO

YES

No liability under OLA 1957

Is the occupier able to show that (s)he is protected by:
- an effective warning;
- a valid exclusion of liability;
- the defence of consent;
- the defence of contributory negligence (which may reduce damages).

— YES

NO →

Occupier is liable under OLA 1957

Assessing liability under the Occupier's Liability Act 1957

3.2 LIABILITY TO TRESPASSERS UNDER THE 1984 ACT

3.2.1 Common law and the duty of common humanity

1. The Occupier's Liability Act 1984 applies mainly to trespassers.
2. Traditionally no real duties were owed at common law except to refrain from inflicting damage intentionally or recklessly:
   a) so no man traps (*Bird v Holbreck* (1828));
   b) some deterrents were accepted (*Clayton v Deane* (1817));
   c) and the law was harsh on children (*Addie & Sons (Colliers) Ltd v Dumbreck* (1927)).
3. So the duty of common humanity developed (*BR Board v Herrington* (1972)).
4. The 1984 Act was passed because of shortcomings in the law.

3.2.2 When the Act applies

1. Like the common duty of humanity, the Act imposes a minimum standard.
2. Under s1(1)(a) the duty to non-visitors is for 'injury ... due to state of premises or things done or omitted to be done on them.'
3. Therefore it does not cover damage to property.
4. 'Occupier' and 'premises' are defined as in the 1957 Act.
5. Under s1(3) the occupier owes a duty if:
   a) (s)he is aware of the danger;
   b) knows or believes that the non-visitor is in danger;
   c) the risk is one against which (s)he should guard.

3.2.3 The nature of the duty

1. Duty by s1(4) is to 'take such care as is reasonable in all the circumstances to prevent injury ... by reason of danger ...'.
2. Standard of care is objective and influenced by type of premises, degree of risk, practicality of precautions, age of trespasser, etc.

3.2.4 Avoiding the duty

1. Warnings
   a) S1(5) says the duty can be discharged by taking 'such steps as are reasonable in the circumstances'.
   b) Warnings are enough for adults (*Westwood v Post Office* (1973));
   c) But children may also require barriers.
2. *Volenti* is preserved as a defence by s1(6) (*Scott and Swainger v Associated British Ports & British Railways Board* (2000)).
3. Exclusion clauses
   a) There is no reference to exclusion clauses, but there is in 1957 Act.
   b) UCTA cannot apply (it never applied to trespassers in the common law before the Act.
   c) As it is a minimum standard there should be no exclusions, but public policy may prevent lawful visitors being worse off than trespassers in non-business premises.

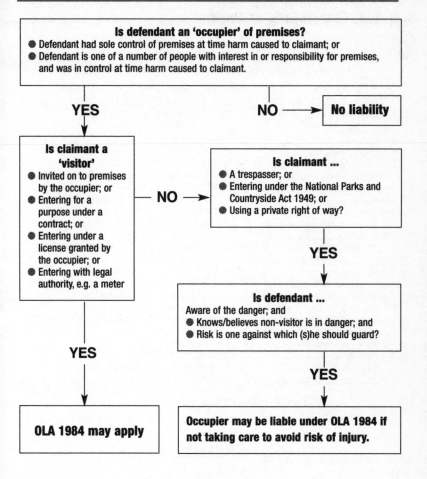

Assessing Liability under the Occupier's Liability Act 1984

Private nuisance – definition and parties

Definition:
continuous, unlawful (unreasonable), indirect interference with a person's enjoyment of land or rights over it.

Potential claimants:
- holder of legal/equitable title;
- landowner not in possession;
- occupier suing for benefit of those affected;
- tenant but not family (*Hunter v Canary Wharf*).

Potential defendants:
- creator of nuisance (*Southport Corporation v Esso Petroleum*);
- person authorising nuisance (*Tetley v Chitty*);
- person who adopts nuisance (*Sedleigh Denfield v O'Callaghan*);
- landlords can be liable to tenants.

Private nuisance – ingredients

Unreasonable use of land
- Locality is important, so what may be a nuisance in a residential area need not be in an industrial area (*Sturges v Bridgman*).
- Nuisance must be continuous (*Bolton v Stone*), although liability possible for an isolated incident arising from a continuous state of affairs (*Spicer v Smee*).
- Locality unimportant if claimant suffers damage (*Halsey v Esso Petroleum*).
- Claimant's over-sensitivity to the nuisance may defeat a claim (*Robinson v Kilvert*).
- Malice can make a legitimate activity unreasonable (*Christie v Davey*) and a deliberate act of malice can be nuisance (*Emmet v Hollywood Silver Fox Farm*).
- A person can 'adopt a nuisance naturally present' (*Leakey v National Trust*).

Indirect interference:
- fumes (*Bliss v Hall*);
- vibrations (*Sturges v Bridgman*).

Enjoyment of land
Pure recreational use not protected (*Bridlington Relay v Yorks Electricity Board*).

NUISANCE

Public nuisance

Something affecting a reasonable class of Her Majesty's citizens materially or in reasonable comfort and convenience of life.

Involves highway and can be:
- obstructions (*Thomas v NUM*);
- projections (*Noble v Harrison*);
- conditions (*Griffiths v Liverpool Corporation*);

but must involve special damage (*Castle v St Augustine Links*).

Private nuisance – defences

- Statutory authority (*Hammersmith Railway v Brand*).
- Planning permission (*Gillingham BC v Medway (Chatham) Dock Ltd*).
- Twenty years prescription (*Sturges v Bridgman*).
- Consent (*Kiddle v City Business Properties*).
- Act of a stranger (*Sedleigh Denfield v O'Callaghan*).
- Public policy (*Miller v Jackson*).

4.1 PRIVATE NUISANCE

4.1.1 The definition, character and purpose of the tort

1. Defined as 'continuous, unlawful and indirect interference with a person's enjoyment of land or some right over, or in connection with it.'
2. It only applies to an 'indirect' interference – direct is trespass.
3. It concerns prevention more than compensation.
4. It concerns the relationship between neighbours.
5. There are three key elements to neighbourhood:
   - continuity – involving a recurring state of affairs;
   - people should be free to use their land as they wish, so long as it does not harm their neighbours;
   - neighbours are subject to many trivial disputes, so there is a risk of the courts being flooded with claims.
6. Only 'unreasonable' interference is a nuisance:
   - so there is no protection against interference classed as reasonable;
   - but if classed as unreasonable it is irrelevant whether it was reasonable for the defendant to engage in such behaviour.
7. The test is: what conduct is sufficient to justify legal intervention?
8. The court must strike a balance between conflicting interests.

4.1.2 Who can sue in nuisance

1. Nuisance usually affects occupiers, so traditionally a claimant is the holder of a legal or equitable title – but might include:
   a) a landowner out of possession;
   b) an occupier suing for the benefit of others affected;
   c) a tenant, but not his/her family:
      - limiting a landlord's responsibility for the state of property (*Habinteng Housing Association v James* (1994));

- so Law Commission Report No 238, 1996 recommends updating the implied covenant of fitness for human habitation in the Landlord and Tenant Act 1985;
- at one point an occupier's family harassed by offensive telephone calls were included (*Khorasandjian v Bush* (1993)), but overruled by (*Hunter v Canary Wharf* (1997)).

4.1.3 The ingredients of the tort

There are three key elements:
a) unlawful use of land;
b) indirect interference with land;
c) indirect interference with the claimant's use or enjoyment of his land.

The unlawful (unreasonable) use of land

1. Interference alone is insufficient – it must be unlawful.
2. Unlawful means unreasonable so, in balancing competing interests, the question is whether in all of the circumstances it is reasonable for the claimant to suffer the particular interference.
3. In assessing the defendant's conduct the court is analysing fault, but in a more flexible way than with negligence – so a defendant might be excused liability for not having the resources to avoid the nuisance (*Solloway v Hampshire County Council* (1981)), but see (*Hurst & another v Hampshire County Council* (1997)) CA.
4. Many key factors are used to assess what is unreasonable.
   a) The locality:
      - The activity may be a nuisance in a residential area but not in an industrial one (*Sturges v Bridgman* (1879)), where vibrations were a nuisance to a doctor's waiting room.
      - So it can include a common facility in the wrong area (*Laws v Florinplace* (1981)).

- The customary use of the area may be a factor (*Sturges v Bridgman* (1879)).
- Locality may be irrelevant if damage is suffered (*St Helens Smelting Co v Tippin* (1865)).
- Courts may in any case try to reach a compromise (*Dunton v Dover D.C.* (1977)).

b) The duration of the interference:
- The interference must be continuous (*Bolton v Stone* (1950)).
- An isolated incident can be a nuisance if arising from a continuous state of affairs (*Spicer v Smee* (1946))
- The cause could be over a long time span (*Cambridge Water Co. v E. Counties Leather PLC* (1994)).
- But very short time spans have been accepted (*Crown River Cruises Ltd v Kimbolton Fireworks Ltd* (1996)).

c) The seriousness of the interference:
- if the claim is for interference with use or enjoyment, the test is whether it is 'an inconvenience materially interfering with the ordinary comfort of human existence, not merely according to elegant or dainty modes and habits of living, but according to plain, sober and simple notions ...' (Knight-Bruce V.C. in (*Walter v Selfe* (1851)).
- Where the claimant suffers physical damage the use of land is unreasonable (*Halsey v Esso Petroleum* (1961)), where smuts from a refinery affecting the claimant's car were a nuisance even though in an industrial area.
- This does not apply if protected by public policy (*Miller v Jackson* (1977)).
- It does not apply if the use of land is an absolute right (*Stephens v Anglian Water Authority* (1987)).
- It does not apply if the activity is seen to be to the public benefit (*Ellison v Ministry of Defence* (1997)).

d) The sensitivity of the claimant if a claimant's own use of land is hypersensitive to the interference he may fail (*Robinson v Kilvert* (1889)).

e) Malice and the conduct of the defendant:
- Malice does play a part in nuisance.
- A deliberately harmful act will normally be a nuisance (*Hollywood Silver Fox Farm v Emmet* (1936)).
- An act of revenge in response to unreasonable behaviour will normally be a nuisance (*Christie v Davey* (1893)).
- Sometimes merely selfish or unthinking behaviour is sufficient (*Tutton v Walter* (1986)).
- Where the defendant does not cause the problem, but, knowing about it allows it to continue is sufficient to be considered nuisance (*Leakey v National Trust* (1980)).

f) The state of the defendant's land:
- A defendant cannot ignore things that may cause interference (*Goldman v Hargrave* (1967)) and (*Leakey v National Trust* (1980)).
- A defendant has a duty to prevent the spread of things that may cause nuisance (*Bradburn v Lindsay* (1983)).

Indirect interference with land

1. Nuisance has included:
- fumes drifting over land (*Bliss v Hall* (1838));
- the loud noise of guns used to frighten breeding silver foxes (*Hollywood Silver Fox Farm v Emmet* (1936));
- vibrations from machinery (*Sturges v Bridgman* (1879));
- hot air rising to an upstairs flat (*Robinson v Kilvert* (1889));
- pollution of rivers (*Pride of Derby Angling Association v British Celanese* (1953)).

The use and enjoyment of land

1. Judges have limited the extent of 'enjoyment' in nuisance.
2. So there is no right to protect pure pleasure or aesthetics (*Bridlington Relay v Yorkshire Electricity Board* (1965)) and, in USA, (*Amphitheatres Inc. v Portland Meadows* (1948)).

3. Confirmed in *Hunter and another v Canary Wharf Ltd* (1997).
4. A functional use supporting pure entertainment or leisure can create liability (*Crown River Cruises Ltd v Kimbolton Fireworks Ltd* (1996)).
5. So lowering the tone of the neighbourhood is not usually actionable but see (*Laws v Florinplace* (1981)).
6. If personal injury is involved the claimant must have a proprietary interest (*Malone v Laskey* (1907)), and see also (*Hunter v Canary Wharf* (1997)).

4.1.4 Who can be sued in nuisance

1. The creator of the nuisance, who does not have to be the occupier (*Southport Corporation v Esso Petroleum* (1953)).
2. A person authorising the nuisance. Compare (*Tetley v Chitty* (1986)) with (*Smith v Scott* (1973)).
3. A person who adopts the nuisance:
   - either of a stranger or trespasser (*Sedleigh Denfield v O'Callaghan* (1940));
   - or of a natural occurrence (*Leakey v National Trust* (1980)).
4. Landlords can be liable to tenants:
   a) for a negligent failure to repair under the usual covenants; or
   b) under the Defective Premises Act 1972; or
   c) from want of repair under the rule in Wringe v Cohen (1940).

4.1.5 Defences

1. Statutory authority:
   - this is the most effective modern defence, since so many activities are licensed (*Hammersmith Railway v Brand* (1869));
   - not available if a discretion is improperly exercised (*Metropolitan Asylum District Hospital v Hill* (1881));

- not available for negligence (*Home Office v Dorset Yacht Co.* (1970));
- unlike Parliament, planning authorities cannot authorise a nuisance except where they have statutory authority to do so. Compare *Wheeler v Sanders* (1995) and (*Gillingham B.C. v Medway (Chatham) Dock Ltd* (1993)).

2. Prescription: this is a defence unique to nuisance – 20 years without complaint and the right to complain lapses (*Sturges v Bridgman*).

3. Act of a stranger or trespasser, but not if adopted (*Sedleigh Denfield v O'Callaghan* (1940)).

4. Consent: e.g. tall building (*Kiddle v City Business Properties Ltd* (1942)).

5. Public policy:
   - both sides should be considered (*Miller v Jackson* (1977));
   - usefulness is insufficient excuse (*Adams v Ursell* (1913)).

6. Coming fresh to the nuisance is no defence (*Bliss v Hall* (1838)).

4.1.6 Remedies

1. Damages.
   a) Test of remoteness is the same as in *Wagon Mound (no 2)* (1961) – foreseeability.
   b) Claimant can recover for physical loss, depreciation in value, and business loss.

2. Injunction:
   a) an order to prevent the nuisance from continuing;
   b) it can be coupled with damages.

3. Abatement of the nuisance:
   a) can involve entering the defendant's property;
   b) but can lead to a counter injunction (*Stanton v Jones* (1995));
   c) and is not always possible (*Burton v Winters* (1993)).

4.1.7 Relationship with other torts

1. Relationship with trespass to land:
    a) the difference is between direct and indirect interference.
    b) repeated trespasses can be nuisances (*Bernstein v Skyways* (1940)).
2. Relationship with (*Rylands v Fletcher* (1868)):
    a) one involves non-natural use of land, the other involves unreasonable use;
    b) before (*Cambridge Water v Eastern Counties Leather* (1994)) there was no requirement for damage to be foreseeable in *R v F*;
    c) nuisance can be committed by a non-occupier, unlike *R v F*;
    d) *R v F*, at least in theory, involves strict liability;
    e) *R v F* covers isolated escapes, nuisance is a continuous state of affairs.
3. Relationship with negligence:
    a) negligence requires the existence of a legal duty;
    b) no claim in negligence for interfering with enjoyment;
    c) nuisance is about creating a balance, but the merest damage in negligence can justify a claim.

4.2 PUBLIC NUISANCE

4.2.1 Definition

1. Unlike private nuisance it extends beyond immediate neighbours.
2. It has been defined as 'something which affects a reasonable class of Her Majesty's citizens materially or in the reasonable comfort and convenience of life.'

4.2.2 Ingredients of the tort

1. A substantial class of people must be involved before an action is possible (*Attorney General v PYA Quarries* (1957)).
2. A claimant must have suffered a special loss over and above other subjects (*Tate & Lyle Industries v GLC* (1983)).
3. Public nuisances can also be crimes by statute.
4. Public nuisance often involves the highway:
   a) obstructions to the highway, e.g. pickets (*Thomas v NUM* (1985));
   b) projections on the highway, e.g. overhanging tree branches providing special damage is caused (*Noble v Harrison* (1926));
   c) condition of the highway; Council may have a duty to maintain it (*Griffiths v Liverpool Corporation* (1967)).
5. Special damage must occur which can be:
   a) personal injuries (*Castle v St Augustine Links* (1922));
   b) damage to goods(*Halsey v Esso Petroleum* (1961));
   c) financial Loss (*Rose v Miles* (1815);
   d) loss of trade connection.

4.3 STATUTORY NUISANCE

1. Parliament has declared certain activities nuisance by statute.
2. They are usually part of public health reform and so prejudicial to health more than prejudicial to land, e.g. Clean Air Act 1956.
3. They provide a means of stopping the nuisance and save the victim the cost and inconvenience of civil action.
4. They are quasi-criminal and enforced by local authorities through the use of abatement notices.
5. Offenders failing to comply are then tried in Magistrates' Court.

CHAPTER 5

STRICT LIABILITY

Ingredients of rule

A bringing on to land and accumulating:

- no liability for things naturally present (*Giles v Walker*);
- or for natural accumulations (*Ellison v Ministry of Defence*);
- escape need not be by thing brought on to land (*Miles v Forest Rock Granite*).

A thing likely to do mischief if it escapes:

- escape need not be probable (*Musgrove v Pandelis*);
- note the thing dangerous in itself (*Shiffman v Order of St John*);
- but escape causes foreseeable harm (*Hale v Jennings*).

A non-natural use of land:

- domestic use is usually natural (*Sokachi v Sas*);
- unusual volume or quantity suggests non-natural use – *The Charing Cross case*.

Thing escapes and causes damage:

- either from land in defendant's control to that not in his control (*Read v Lyons*);
- or from circumstances within defendant's control to ones not in his control (*British Celanese v A H Hunt*);
- damage is foreseeable (*Cambridge Water v Eastern Counties Leather*).

Parties to an action

Potential defendants.

- If (*Read v Lyons*) is followed will be owners or occupiers of land thing escaped from.
- If *British Celanese v Hunt* is taken will be people in control of circumstances escape happened from.

Potential claimants.

- If (*Read v Lyons*) is followed then owners/occupiers of land thing escapes to.
- If *British Celanese* then claimant does not need a proprietary interest in land.
- See also (*Crown River Cruises v Kimbolton Fireworks*).

RYLANDS V FLETCHER

Problems with rule:

- Numbers of defences.
- Requirement of foreseeability.
- (*Read v Lyons*).
- Non-natural use.
- No real strict liability for dangers.

Defences

- Consent (*Peters v Prince of Wales Theatre*).
- Common benefit (*Dunne v North West Gas Board*).
- Act of stranger (*Perry v Dendricks Transport*).
- Act of God (*Nicholls v Marsland*).
- Statutory authority (*Green v Chelsea Waterworks*).
- Contributory negligence (*Eastern Telegraph v Capetown Tramways*).

5.1 THE RULE IN RYLANDS V FLETCHER

5.1.1 The Definition, purpose, and character of the rule.

1. First defined by Blackburn. J. In Court of Exchequer Chamber in the case: 'the person who, for purposes of his own, brings on his land, and collects and keeps there anything likely to do mischief if it escapes, must keep it in at his peril, and, if he does not do so, he is prima facie answerable for all the damage which is the natural consequence of its escape.'

2. Lord Cairns in HL added requirement of non-natural use of land.

3. The tort is said to be one of strict liability, but it is possible to argue it as a type of nuisance used to cover isolated escapes.

   - There are many defences available, so it is strict liability only in the sense that the claimant need not prove fault.
   - If the use of land is natural an action will fail.
   - It was previously distinguished from nuisance which required foreseeability, where *Rylands v Fletcher* did not.
   - Now (*Cambridge Water Co. v Eastern Counties Leather plc* (1994)) suggests that foreseeability is required.
   - Judges have limited strict liability by restricting the use of the rule – to escapes from land only (*Read v Lyons* (1947)) and to 'special use of land bringing with it increased danger to others' (*Rickards v Lothian* (1913)), and see also (*Cambridge Water and Crown River Cruises v Kimbolton* (1996)).
   - Claimants have recovered even though not occupiers of land, so it is not a straightforward extension of nuisance.

5.1.2 The ingredients of the rule

1. There are four key ingredients to the tort:
   a) a bringing on to land;
   b) of a thing which is likely to do mischief if it escapes;
   c) which amounts to a non-natural use of land;
   d) the thing actually escapes, causing damage.

A bringing on to land

1. If thing is naturally present on land there can be no liability (*Giles v Walker* (1890)) and (*Pontardawe R.D.C v Moore-Gwyn* (1929)).
2. There is no liability where the thing naturally accumulates (*Elision v Ministry of Defence* (1997)).
3. But nuisance may be possible (*Leakey v National Trust* (1980)).
4. The person bringing the thing on to the land need not be the owner or occupier of the land (*Charing Cross Electricity Supply Co. v Hydraulic Power Co.* (1914)) (*The Charing Cross Case*).
5. The defendant must have had a purpose for bringing the thing on to the land, but it need not have been for his/her benefit. Compare (*Smeaton v Ilford Corporation* (1954)) with (*Dunne v North Western Gas Board* (1964)).
6. The escape can be of something other than the thing brought on to the land (*Miles v Forest Rock Granite Co.* (1917)), where explosives used in blasting caused rock to escape.

A thing likely to do mischief if it escapes

1. Escape need not be probable (*Musgrove v Pandelis* (1919)).
2. The thing need not be dangerous in itself (*Shiffman v Order of St John* (1936)), where the thing was a flag pole.
3. It must be a source of foreseeable harm if it does escape (*Hale v Jennings Bros.* (1938)), where a 'chairoplane' car flew off the ride in a fairground.
4. Even people have been held as dangerous (*A.G. v Corke* (1933)).

A non-natural use of land

1. This was added by Lord Cairns in HL: 'if the defendants, not stopping at the natural use of their close, had desired to use it for any purpose I may term a non-natural use ... and in consequence ... the water came to escape ... it appears to me that which the defendants were doing they were doing at their own peril...'.

2. It was developed and explained by Lord Moulton in *Rickards v Lothian* (1913): 'not every use of land brings into play this principle. It must be some special use bringing with it increased danger to others, and not merely by the ordinary use of land or such as is proper for the general benefit of the community.'

3. Non-natural use is a fluid concept inevitably changing with technological developments.

4. It is 'extraordinary' use rather than 'artificial' use.

5. Domestic use is usually natural, e.g. *Sokachi v Sas* (1947)) – fire; (*Collingwood v Home & Colonial Stores Ltd* (1936)) – electricity; *Rickards v Lothian* (1913) – water pipes.

6. Sometimes also applies to commercial premises (*Peters v Prince of Wales Theatre (Birmingham) Ltd* (1943)).

7. Unusual volume or quantity indicates non-natural use (*The Charing Cross Case*).

8. Technical developments may be non-natural while at an innovative stage (*Musgrove v Pandelis* (1919)).

9. Context may also make them non-natural (*Mason v Levy Autoparts of England* (1967)).

10. If a public benefit is gained from the activity it may make it a natural use (*British Celanese v A.H. Hunt* (1969)).

11. Things connected with war may be a natural use even in peace time (*Ellison v Ministry of Defence* (1997)).

12. Some activities will be seen as a non-natural use despite being of public benefit, e.g. use of chemicals (*Cambridge Water* (1994)).

The thing must actually escape and cause damage

1. Blackburn's original rule was not rigidly restricted to neighbouring landowners (he probably intended a general liability for dangerous activities.

2. The rule was limited by Lord MacMillan in *Read v Lyons* (1947): 'the rule derives from a conception of mutual duties of adjoining landowners ...'.
3. It was also limited by Lord Simons in *Read v Lyons* by defining escape as 'from a place where the defendant has occupation or control over land to a place which is outside of his occupation or control.'
4. However, escape is also defined as 'from a set of circumstances over which the defendant has control to a set where he does not.' by Lawton J. in *British Celanese v A H Hunt* (1969).

5.1.3 The parties to an action

1. A defendant in an action will be either:
   - according to Lord Simon in *Read v Lyons* an owner or an occupier who satisfies the four requirements; or
   - according to Lawton J. in *British Celanese* a person where the escape is from a set of circumstances under his control to one which is not.
2. Possible claimants also vary according to the judge:
   - Blackburn J. suggested there is no need for the claimant to have a proprietary interest.
   - Lord MacMillan in *Read v Lyons* said there is.
   - Lawton J. in *British Celanese* was not prepared to limit the rule that much, so that a claimant could even be a party who has suffered personal injury.
   - Recently a claim has succeeded where the escape was from the defendant's control of the highway on to the claimant's land (*Rigby v Chief Constable of Northamptonshire* (1985).
   - Another successful claim is an escape from accumulations in a vessel escaping on to other vessels (*Crown River Cruises Ltd v Kimbolton Fireworks Ltd* (1996)).

5.1.4 Recoverable loss and remoteness of damage

1. According to MacMillan, recovery is only possible for damage to land occupied by the claimant or his chattels on that land.
2. Lawton suggests claims for personal injury are also possible (*Hale v Jennings* (1938)).
3. A successful action for economic loss is less likely (*Weller v Foot and Mouth Disease Research Unit* (1966)).
4. The tort is not actionable *per se*, so damage must be proved.
5. So there is no liability for mere interference with enjoyment of land as there is in nuisance (*Eastern & SA Telegraph Co. v Cape Town Tramways Co.* (1902)).
6. By *Cambridge Water* the defendant must know or ought reasonably to foresee that damage of the relevant kind might be a consequence of the escape (this is remoteness as in negligence and seems inconsistent with strict liability.

5.1.5 Possible defences

1. **Consent:** e.g. occupiers of tall buildings (*Peters v Prince of Wales Theatre* (1943)).
2. **Common benefit:** no liability if source of danger is kept for both defendant and claimant (*Dunne v North West Gas Board* (1964)).
3. **Act of a stranger:** if stranger over whom defendant exercises no control causes the escape then no liability (*Perry v Kendricks Transport Ltd* (1956)), but see (*Mehta v Union of India* (1987)).
4. **Act of God:** will only succeed for conditions of nature 'which no human foresight can provide against ...', e.g. extreme weather conditions (*Nichols v Marsland* (1876)).
5. **Statutory authority:** if the escape is a direct result of carrying out the duty (*Green v Chelsea Waterworks Co.* (1894)).
6. **Contributory negligence**: damages reduced if claimant is

partly at fault for the escape (*Eastern & SA Telegraph Co. v Cape Town Tramways* (1902)).

5.1.6 Problems with the rule

1. Often seen merely as an extension of nuisance, so there is no general strict liability for hazardous activities.
2. The principle has been constantly limited in scope:
   ● requirement of non-natural use;
   ● *Read v Lyons* reasoning on escape;
   ● the breadth of defences available;
   ● the requirement of foreseeability in *Cambridge Water*;
   ● reluctance to expand the principle in *Crown River Cruises*.
3. Has doubtful modern relevance:
   ● most instances could be covered by negligence;
   ● rarely used now, and rarely successfully;
   ● since *Cambridge Water* the Australian High Court has abolished the rule saying it was effectively swallowed up by negligence (*Burnie Port Authority v General Jones Pty Land* (1994));
   ● many areas concerning hazards are now covered by statute (*Blue Circle Industries plc v Ministry of Defence* (1998)).

5.2 LIABILITY FOR ANIMALS

5.2.1 Introduction

1. The origins of liability are in medieval law:
   a) animals were a major source of wealth so attitudes differed;
   b) animals had a separate system because they are mobile (a 'will of their own').
2. There were two basic actions in the common law:
   a) scienter (knowingly keeping a dangerous animal that escaped and caused harm;
   b) cattle trespass (damage caused by escaping livestock.
3. The Animals Act 1971 replaced these, retaining the essentials.

4. Other torts can be used where the Act does not apply.
5. The Pearson Committee found that animals are responsible for 50,000 injuries annually, but few actions are brought.

Origins and common law actions
Liability began in Middle Ages:
- scienter – keeping a dangerous animal that escapes and causes harm;
- cattle trespass – damage caused by escaping livestock.

Liability still under many torts:
- trespass to goods (*Manton v Brocklebank*);
- private nuisance (*Rapier v London Tramways*);
- *Rylands v Fletcher* (*Brady v Warren*);
- negligence (*Birch v Mills*);
- very appropriate if Act ineffective (*Draper v Hodder*).

Animals Act 1971 – liability
Dangerous species:
- defined in s6(2) – animal not commonly domesticated in UK and with characteristics that, unless restricted, likedly to cause severe damage or any damage caused likely to be severe;
- dangerous is a question of fact in each case (*Behrens v Bertram Mills Circus*);
- keeper is strictly liable;
- a keeper is either the owner or head of a household in which a person under 16 is the owner.

Non-dangerous species:
- duty is under s2(2);
- keeper liable if:
  i) damage of a kind animal is likely to cause unless restrained, or if caused by animal is likely to be severe;
  ii) likelihood or severity of damage is due to characteristics of individual animal or species, or of species at specific times;
  iii) keeper knows of characteristics.

ANIMALS

Animals Act (defences
- S5(1) – damage due entirely to fault of victim (*Sylvester v Chapman*).
- S5(2) – victim voluntarily accepted risk (*Cummings v Grainger*).
- S5(3) – animal either not kept for protection or, if so, then reasonable to do so (*Cummings v Grainger*).
- S10 – contributory negligence.

5.2.2 Common law torts

1. If the requirements of any tort are met an action is possible e.g.:
   - trespass to goods (*Manton v Brocklebank* (1923));
   - trespass to land (*League Against Cruel Sports v Scott* (1985));
   - private nuisance (*Rapier v London Tramways* (1893));
   - *Rylands v Fletcher* (*Brady v Warren* (1900));

- defamation, e.g. a parrot taught to repeat insulting untruths;
- assault and battery, e.g. a dog trained to attack;
- with more widespread application, negligence for a failure to control an animal where some risk of harm is foreseeable (*Gomberg v Smith* (1962)) and (*Birch v Mills* (1995));
- negligence is useful in respect of non-dangerous species where the Act may prove ineffective (*Draper v Hodder* (1972));
- so a duty to take reasonable precautions against foreseeable risks exists (*Smith v Prendergast* (1984)).

2. Liability can exist simultaneously in more than one tort (*Pitcher v Martin* (1937)).

5.2.3 The Animals Act 1971

Dangerous Species (*ferae naturae*)

1. By s6(2) a dangerous species is one:
  (i) which is not commonly domesticated in the UK;
  (ii) where fully grown animals usually have such characteristics that they are likely, unless restricted, to cause severe damage, or any damage they cause is likely to be severe.

2. Under s2(1) the 'keeper' of a dangerous species is liable.

3. Dangerous is a question of law not fact (*Behrens v Bertram Mills Circus* (1957)).
  - So it could include species domesticated in other countries.
  - Few native species correspond to the category.
  - Dangerous even if unlikely to do harm if possible harm would be severe (*Tutin v Chipperfield Promotions* (1980)).
  - So liability is strict.

4. Keeper is defined in s6(3) as:
  (i) an owner or possessor; or
  (ii) the head of a household of which a member under 16 possesses the animal.

  N.B. It is possible to have more than one keeper.

5. Dangerous Wild Animals Act 1976 requires licensing of animals, and third party insurance.

Non-dangerous species (*mansuetae naturae*)

1. There is a rather complex duty under s2(2). Keeper is liable if:

a) the damage is of a kind which the animal is likely to cause unless restrained, or which if caused by the animal is likely to be severe;

b) the likelihood or severity of damage was due to unusual characteristics of the individual animal, or common in species only at particular times;

c) those characteristics were known to the keeper, or a person having charge of the animal who is a member of the household and is under 16.

2. The subsection requires proper interpretation, which is to consider each part in turn (*Curtis v Betts* (1990)).

- So, by s2(2)(a) damage need not be caused in the way which is likely (*Smith v Ainger* (1990)).
- S2(2)(a) might include infectious animals.
- S2(2)(b) distinguishes between permanent and temporary characteristics, and between species and breed (*Smith v Ainger and Cummings v Grainger* (1977)).
- 'Likelihood of damage' refers to the individual animal.
- 'Likely to be severe' refers to the possible injury (*Cummings v Grainger*) and (*Curtis v Betts*).
- 'Knowledge in s2(2)(c) means actual knowledge.
- Implied knowledge may be negligence (*Draper v Hodder*).
- There must be a causal link between the characteristics of the animal and the damage it inflicts (*Jaundrill v Gillett* (1996)).

Defences

1. By s5(1) a keeper is not liable for damage 'due wholly to the fault of the person suffering it' (*Sylvester v Chapman* (1935)).

2. By s5(2) there is no liability 'for a person who has voluntarily accepted the risk' (*Cummings v Grainger* (1977)), where a woman entered a scrap yard already afraid of the Alsatian dog guarding it.

3. By s5(3) the keeper is not liable to a trespasser if the animal was not kept for protection of property, or if it was it was reasonable to do so (*Cummings v Grainger*), but see now also the Guard Dogs Act 1995

4. By s10 can apportion damages if contributory negligence shown.

Trespassing livestock

1. S11 defines livestock as 'cattle, horses, asses, mules, hinnies, sheep, pigs, goats, poultry and deer in the wild state'.

2. 'Cattle trespass' is replaced by s4, imposing liability if animals stray and:
   - damage is done to land or property; or
   - expenses incurred in keeping them till restored to the owner.

3. Possible defences are:
   - s5(1) if the damage is wholly due to the fault of the claimant;
   - s10 apportionment for contributory negligence;
   - s5(5) if driving livestock on to highway only liable if negligent;
   - s5(6) there is no general duty to fence the land, but if there is a customary duty then a failure to fence provides a defence compare (*Tillet v Ward* (1882)) with (*Matthews v Wicks* (1987));
   - s7 power to detain straying animal till damage is paid for. Must notify police within 48 hours; can sell after 14 days.

Liability for injury to livestock by dogs

1. By s3 a keeper is liable if a dog kills or injures livestock.

2. No need to show abnormal characteristics, so greater protection than for people.

3. Straying of livestock on to land where a dog is entitled to be may be a defence under s 5(4).

4. Defences under s5(1) and s10 are also available.

5. By s9 it is legal to kill a dog if it is to protect livestock.

- The dog must be worrying and there is no other way of dealing with it, or it has not left the vicinity.
- Must be entitled to protect livestock and must notify the police within 48 hours.

Animals straying onto the highway

1. Prior to the Act there was no liability.

2. S8(1) abolished immunity and introduced liability in negligence.

3. By s8(2) no liability for putting animals on unfenced land if:

    (i) the land is common, or a customary right not to fence, or town or village green;

    (ii) there is a right to put the animal there.

4. Duty is only to do what is reasonable not, for example, to fence a moor.

5. Registration of Commons Act 1971 requires registration of rights to graze on common.

Remoteness of Damage

1. Not dealt with by the Act, so common law applies.

2. Liability for animals is like (*Rylands v Fletcher*) – this was excluded from the *Wagon Mound* foreseeability test, so probably the direct consequence test applies instead.

3. S2(1) in any case refers to liability being for 'any damage'.

4. By s2(2) for non-dangerous species damages are limited to those resulting from unusual characteristics known to the keeper.

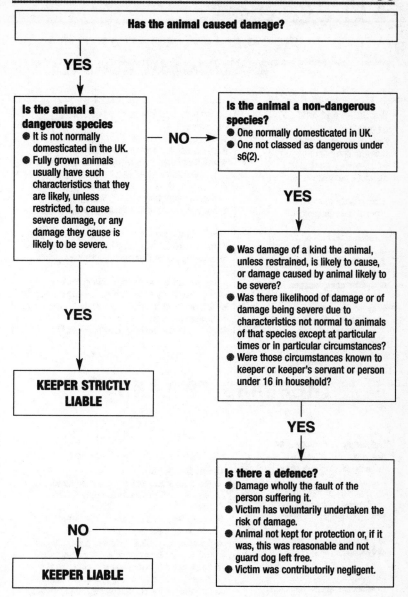

Liability for dangerous and non-dangerous species under the Animals Act 1971

CHAPTER 6

TRESPASS TO LAND

Definition and purpose of tort

Defined as: intentional unlawful entry or direct interference with land in another's possession.

Actionable *per se*, so no proof of damage needed.

Purpose of action can be:
- to remove intruders;
- to settle disputes over title;
- to seek compensation for loss or damage;
- to recover land when unlawfully ejected.

Claimants and types of trespass
Claimants:
- based on possession;
- so lessees and mortgagees can sue;
- and a squatter can sue against someone with less title (*Graham v Peat*);
- but not a possessor against someone with superior title (*Delaney v TP Smith*);
- nor a lodger against a landlord (*White v Bayley*).

Types of trespass:
- requires direct entry onto land (*Perera v Andiyar*);
- but need not be defendant who enters (*Smith v Stone*);
- can be active interference (*Basely v Clarkson*);
- or static interference (*Kelsen v Imperial Tobacco*);
- and can be only temporary (*Woolerton & Wilson v Richard Costain*);
- or the merest touching (*Westripp v Baldock*).

TRESPASS TO LAND

Defences and remedies
Defences:
- customary right to enter (*Mercer v Denne*);
- common law right to enter (*Clissold v Cratchley*);
- statutory right to enter;
- *volenti*;
- necessity;
- licenses.

Remedies:
- injunction and/or damages;
- distress damage feasant;
- declaration (*Acxton BC v Morris*).

Definition of land
- *Cujus est solum ejus est usque ad coleum et ad inferos* – includes air space above and soil below.
- Covers air space to a reasonable extent (*Kelsen v Imperial Tobacco*).
- Does not cover air to extent of preventing air traffic (*Lord Bernstein of Leigh v Skyways*).
- Can prevent unlawful use of a public road over a person's land (*Harrison v Duke of Rutland*).
- Can include the boundary of the land (*Westripp v Baldock*).
- Most air rights now covered by CAA, and undersoil rights also by statute.

6.1 THE ORIGINS AND CHARACTER OF TRESPASS

1. Trespass is as old as the common law itself.
2. It was necessary so claimants could bring their own action where the distinction between civil and criminal law was unclear.
3. Derives from the Latin: *trans* (through) and *passus* (a pace).
4. It is most accurately used in conjunction with land.
5. But there are torts of trespass to the person and to goods also.
6. It is used generally to refer to an interference.
7. It is actionable *per se* (so without proof of damage).
8. Originally it was only actionable if it arose directly as a consequence of the defendant's direct and positive act.
9. Indirect interference or omission would be an action on the case (forerunner of negligence) when damage had to be shown.

6.2 TRESPASS TO LAND

6.2.1 Definition, character and purpose of the tort

1. Developed from the writ *quare clausum fregit* by way of the taking of an enclosed area.
2. Defined as the intentional or negligent, unlawful entry upon or direct interference with the land in another's possession.
3. The tort is actionable *per se*, so no proof of damage needed.
4. Damages are payable if there is any loss.
5. It can be intentional, but also by a person who enters lawfully, but then carries out an unlawful act.
6. There may be many purposes of suing:
   - to remove unwanted intruders;
   - to settle disputes over title;
   - to seek compensation for loss or damage;
   - to recover land from which claimant was unlawfully ejected.

7. The action can be by a possessor rather than an owner.

6.2.2 Potential claimants

1. If the tort were based only on title a tenant could not claim. If it was based on pure possession then an owner might not claim.
2. So, an action is in favour of the person in possession at the time the trespass is committed, as against the wrongdoer.
3. So 'possession is title as against a wrongdoer ...'.
4. An action is available to lessees, mortgagees, etc., and possession need not be legal, i.e. a squatter may sue a trespassing third party (*Graham v Peat* (1861)).
5. But not the superior owner (*Delaney v T.P. Smith & Co.* (1946)).
6. Possession means exclusivity, so a lessee can sue a lessor, but a lodger may not sue the landlord (*White v Bayley* (1861)).
7. However, a licensee may gain a proprietary interest as in estoppel.

6.2.3 Actions amounting to a trespass

1. Acts/non-acts must be direct; indirect interference is actionable, as nuisance or negligence (*Lemon v Webb* (1894)), and (*Esso Petroleum Co. Southport Corporation* (1956)).
2. There must be an entry on to the land (*Perera v Andiyar* (1953)).
3. It need not be the defendant who enters (*Smith v Stone* (1647)).
4. So, it might be rocks or balls thrown, but not rubbish blown by the wind compare (*Smith v Stone* (1647)) with *Esso v Southport Corp.* (1956).
5. Any presence can be a trespass, e.g. walking, standing, riding.
6. So it can be active interference (*Basely v Clarkson* (1681)).
7. It can also be a static intrusion (*Kelsen v Imperial Tobacco Co.* (1956)).

8. Can be merely temporary (*Woolerton & Wilson v Richard Costain Ltd* (1970)), where a crane swung over the claimant's land.

9. The merest contact can be trespass (*Westripp v Baldock* (1938)).

10. A trespass can occur even if the original entry was lawful.

6.2.4 Definition of land in trespass

1. There is no single concept. Traditional proposition is *cujus est solum ejus est usque ad coleum et ad inferos* (the action extends to the air above the land and the sub-soil beneath it.

2. It can be the land, any part of the land, any structure on the land.

3. It can even be the boundary (*Westripp v Baldock* (1938)).

4. Most underground rights are now under statutory authority.

- Rights can extend under roads to include unlawful use of the road (*Harrison v The Duke of Rutland* (1893)) and *Hickman v Maisey* (1900).

- But cannot extend to adjoining land (*Randall v Tarrant* (1955)).

5. Air space:

   a) overhanging signs have been trespass (*Kelsen v Imperial Tobacco* (1956)) and (*Gifford v Dent* (1926)).

   b) wire cables (*Wandsworth Board of Works v United Telephones* (1864)).

   c) cranes (*Woolerton & Wilson v Richard Constain* (1970)).

   d) but not balloons flying overhead (*Pickering v Rudd* (1815)) and (*Saunders v Smith* (1838)).

   e) aircraft are unlikely to amount to a trespass (*Lord Bernstein of Leigh v Skyways General Ltd* (1977)), where there was no liability in trespass when aerial photographs were taken of Lord Bernstein's estate.;

   f) aircraft in any case have free passage under the Civil Aviation Act 1982.

6.2.5 Trespass ab initio

1. A common law doctrine – if a person enters land lawfully then does an act inconsistent with his rights, then the entry is deemed unlawful from the beginning despite his original lawful entry.
2. Needed to stop abuses by lawful visitors (*Oxley v Watts* (1785)).
3. It may be ineffective if a lawful purpose remains (*Elias v Pasmore* (1934)).
4. Possibly the doctrine is no longer in existence according to CA. (*Chic Fashions Ltd v Jones* (1968)).

6.2.6 Defences

1. A customary right to enter (*Mercer v Denne* (1905)), where the defendant was prevented from building on his beach because fishermen had an ancient right to dry their nets on it.
2. A common law right to enter, which is lost if the person entering goes beyond his legal rights (*Clissold v Cratchley* (1910)).
3. Statutory right to enter, e.g. police under PACEA 1984; meter readers by Rights of Entry (Gas and Electricity Boards) Act 1954.
4. *Volenti non fit injuria* (where visitors are allowed on to land.
5. Necessity, e.g. someone rescuing a child from a burning building.
6. Licenses – constantly given e.g. shops etc – valid only while terms of licence are complied with.

6.2.7 Remedies

1. If claimant is in possession (s)he can sue for damage resulting from infringement and injunction to prevent further trespass.
2. If defendant is in possession claimant can sue for ejectment for recovery of land, possibly with mesne profits.

3. Damages may be:
  a) nominal and exemplary;
  b) related to actual deterioration;
  c) related to the cost of repossession.
4. Other remedies:
  a) distress damage feasant – keeping an object causing damage
  b) declaration – if rights are uncertain (*Acton B.C. v Morris* (1953)).

	Private nuisance	**Public nuisance**	***Rylands v Fletcher***	**Trespass to land**
Claimants	Person with proprietary interest in land	A member of a class of Her Majesty's citizens	A person harmed by the escape	Person in possession of land
Defendants	Landowner, creator, person adopting nuisance	Person creating nuisance	Person in control of land from which thing escapes	Person carrying out the trespass
Duration of interference	Must be continuous	Single interference is enough	Single escape is enough	A single trespass is enough
Directness of interference	Must be indirect	Could be direct or indirect	Could be direct or indirect	Must be direct
Need to prove fault	Requires unreasonable use of land – which is indirect	Fault need not be proved	*Cambridge Water* says foreseeability required – suggests fault	Actionable *per se* – so no need to prove fault
Locality of interference	Relevant unless damage caused	Could be relevant, e.g. to losing client connection	Could be relevant in deciding what is non-natural	Not relevant
Availability of damages	Physical harm, personal injury to proprietor, economic loss	Physical harm, personal injury, economic loss	Physical loss and personal injury	Any damage related to the trespass – and no need to show damage
Defences	Statutory authority, prescription, consent, act of stranger, public policy, over-sensitivity of claimant	General defences	Consent, common benefit, act of a stranger, or Act of God, statutory authority, contributory negligence	Customary right to enter, common law right, statutory right, consent, necessity, license
Whether also a crime	No – unless statutory	Yes – can be	No	Yes possible under some statutes

The similarities and differences between the torts relating to land

CHAPTER 7

TORTS CONCERNING GOODS

Trespass to goods
Defined as – direct, immediate, intentional interference with personal property belonging to another.
● Interference must be direct (*Fouldes v Willoughby*).
● Contact with goods must be intentional (*Ranson v Kitner*).
Claimants are those entitled to immediate possession.

Conversion
More complex because it involves ownership as well as possession.
Defined as – intentional, wrongful interference of substantial nature with claimant's possession or rights to possession, or dealing with goods in manner inconsistent with rights of owner.
Can be:
● wrongly taking with intention to keep goods permanently;
● destroying or misusing goods (*Moorgate Mercantile v Finch*);
● selling goods;
● refusing to return goods when asked (*Arthur v Anker*).

TRESPASS TO GOODS

Torts (Interference with Goods) Act 1977
Made a number of changes to the law.
● The right to sue for negligent loss by a bailee is conversion.
● Created general liability for interference and remedies.
● Contributory negligence was removed as a defence.
● Rules introduced regarding disposal of unclaimed goods.
● Claiming sum for improvements to goods whilst in wrongful possession made possible by the Act.
● Old rule that defendant not allowed to plead a third party had better title to the goods than claimant was reversed.

Remedies
Trespass:
● damages or
● injunction.
Conversion:
● delivery of goods plus damages for consequential loss;
● or full value of goods plus consequential loss.

7.1 TRESPASS TO GOODS

7.1.1 Introduction

1. Trespass, meaning interference, is one of the oldest areas of tort.

2. Trespass to goods developed alongside trespass to land and to the person, and was similar but protected personal property.
3. Medieval law became outdated and in need of reform, so updated and clarified in Torts (Interference with Goods) Act 1977, but not entirely, so some common law still remains, adding confusion.

7.1.2 Trespass to goods

1. One of the original two torts to do with goods.
2. Defined as 'direct, immediate interference with personal property belonging to another person …'.
3. Claimants are those entitled to immediate possession.
4. Interference must be direct (*Fouldes v Willoughby* (1841)).
5. The interference must be intentional in the sense that contact with the goods is intentional (*Ranson v Kitner* (1888)).
6. Traditionally actionable *per se* (without proof of damage), but this probably does not survive (*Letang v Cooper* (1965)).
7. Under s11(1) Torts (Interference with Goods) Act 1977 the defence of contributory negligence is not available.
8. Wheel clamping can be a trespass unless the claimant voluntarily undertook the risk of the clamping (*Vine v Waltham Forest London Borough Council* (2000)), where the claimant had not seen warning signs and did not appreciate the consequences of trespassing.

7.1.3 Conversion

1. Trespass to goods is a fairly simple tort; conversion is complex.
   a) This is because it involves ownership as well as possession.
   b) As it takes many forms it is often said to defy easy definition.
2. Broadly defined as 'intentional, wrongful interference of a substantial nature with the claimant's possession or right to possession of the goods …'; or 'dealing with goods in a

manner inconsistent with the true owner's rights …'. So it might occur even where the defendant has no knowledge that the goods belong to the claimant (*Lewis v Avery* (1972)).

3. There are a number of examples of conversion:
   - wrongfully taking the goods with the intention of keeping them permanently, or at least for some time;
   - selling the goods or assisting in their disposition;
   - destroying or misusing the goods (*Moorgate Mercantile Co. v Finch* (1962));
   - refusing to return the goods once their return has been demanded (*Arthur v Anker* (1996)) (wheel clamping).

4. After the Act a verbal statement denying the claimant's title is not conversion.

5. Again the Act removes contributory negligence as a defence.

7.1.4 Other common law provisions

1. The Act abolished a third common law action (part of conversion).

2. In all three torts there was no remedy for a claimant who did not have possession or an immediate right to possession of the goods.

3. So common law developed an action on the case (as in land) to challenge interference with the claimant's reversionary interest in the goods.

7.1.5 The Torts (Interference with Goods) Act 1977

1. The Act tried to remove overlaps and ambiguities with common law.

2. It did make a number of changes to the law:
   - the right to sue for negligent loss by a bailee is conversion;
   - created general liability for interference and remedies;
   - contributory negligence was removed as a defence;
   - rules were introduced regarding disposal of unclaimed goods;

- claiming a sum for improvements made to the goods whilst in wrongful possession was made possible by the Act;
- the old rule that the defendant was not allowed to plead that a third party had better title to the goods than the claimant was reversed.

7.1.6 Remedies

1. In trespass to goods the claimant may recover damages or an injunction.
2. Conversion has been modified by the Act with two possibilities:
   - delivery of the goods, plus damages for consequential loss;
   - if this is not possible or appropriate then the claimant can have the full value of the goods, plus damages for any consequential loss.

Common law liability
- Comes from case of *Donoghue v Stevenson*.
- Manufacturers now includes wholesalers, retailers, etc.
- Claimants are 'ultimate consumers', e.g. includes people receiving gifts (*Stennet v Hancock*).
- Must show breach of duty as well as duty (*Grant v Australian Knitting Mills*).
- Must show causation (*Evans v Triples Safety Glass*).
- Can recover for defects but not pure loss of value (*Muirhead v Industrial Tank*).

PRODUCT LIABILITY

Criticisms of Act
- Does not apply to all products, defects or damage.
- Strict limitation period.
- Does not apply to disputes pre-1988.
- Too many defences.
- More like negligence than strict liability.

Consumer Protection Act 1987
Introduced to give effect to EU Directive 85/374. Civil liability is imposed in s2(1).

Defendants:
- producers – including manufacturers, those abstracting the product or adding to it in an industrial process;
- importers, suppliers (e.g. retailers) and 'own branders';
- anyone else in chain of manufacture or distribution.

Products covered:
- goods – anything growing or any ship, aircraft, vehicle;
- products – goods, parts of other products, but not buildings and nuclear power.

Defects covered:
- if safety is not such as persons are generally entitled to expect.

Types of damage covered:
- death and personal injury, loss or damage to property;
- but not damage under £275, business property, damage to the defective property itself.

Limitation:
- within three years of becoming aware of defect, damage, or identity of defendant;
- ten years from date of knowledge for latent damage.

Possible defences:
- product complies with statute or EU;
- defect did not exist when supplied;
- not supplied in course of business;
- defendant did not supply product;
- state of technological or scientific knowledge when goods supplied.

7.2 PRODUCT LIABILITY

7.2.1 Introduction

1. Product liability is only one aspect of consumer protection.
2. Its origins are in contract law:
   a) *caveat emptor* traditionally applied;
   b) effective consumer protection began with the Sale of Goods Act 1893, which implied terms as to quality of the goods into contracts.
3. Otherwise only limited opportunities existed to sue in tort in respect of dangerous goods.
4. Suing in contract had obvious shortcomings:
   - remedies were only available to the parties to the contract;
   - damages limited to loss of bargain, reliance loss, restitution.
5. So a doctrine of tortious liability for defective goods developed.

7.2.2 Common law liability for defective products in tort

1. Came from Lord Atkin's judgement in *Donoghue v Stevenson* (1932) 'a manufacturer of products ... he intends to reach the ultimate consumer in the form in which they left him with no reasonable possibility of ... examination ... and knowledge that absence of reasonable care ... will result in an injury to consumer's life or property, owes a duty to the consumer to take reasonable care ...'.
2. Not concerned with quality of goods, but damage they cause:
   - damage must be physical, not purely economic (*Murphy v Brentwood DC* (1990));
   - concerns over quality are contested in contract law.
3. At first applied to foodstuffs only, but later extended to anything manufactured (*Grant v Australian Knitting Mills* (1936)) (liability when underpants still containing a chemical caused dermatitis in the wearer).

4. Potential defendants are 'manufacturers' – a narrow concept, but expanded to include wholesalers, retailers, repairers, hirers, and assemblers (if under a duty to inspect the goods).

5. Potential claimants are any 'ultimate consumers'.
   - Again this is a broad concept including anyone who the 'manufacturer' should see as being affected by his actions.
   - It can be people receiving goods as presents, borrowing goods, or innocent bystanders (*Stennet v Hancock* (1939)).

6. Bringing an action is the same as for negligence:
   a) The claimant must show a duty of care, breach, and a causal link with the damage suffered.
   b) Breach is, for example, a failure in the production process (*Grant v Australian Knitting Mills* (1936)) – and can include failing to do anything about a known fault (*Walton v British Leyland* (1978)). Detailed knowledge of manufacturing processes is beyond the capability of most consumers, placing a very heavy burden of proof, so the doctrine *res ipsa loquitur* may be appropriate.
   c) Causation will also only be proved if:
      - there is no other cause for the defects in the product, so the chain of distribution can be a problem for the claimant (*Evans v Triplex Safety Glass* (1936));
      - there is no negligent inspection of the goods by claimant which should have revealed the defect (*Griffiths v Arch Engineering Co.* (1968)).
   d) Can recover for damage caused by defects in goods (*Aswan Engineering Establishment Co. v Lupdine Ltd* (1987)).
   e) Cannot recover a pure loss of value in the goods themselves (*Muirhead v Industrial Tank Specialities Ltd* (1985)).

7. Clearly the two most important problems of the tort are:
   - the difficulty of proving causation;
   - the difficulty of establishing fault.

   The Thalidomide cases (settled out of court) are evidence of this.

7.2.3 The Consumer Protection Act 1987

Introduction

1. The Act was UK's response to EU Directive 85/374 on product liability requiring harmonization of member states law.

2. The Act is both criminal and civil in content:
   - in the regulatory sense it has been supplemented by the Product Safety Regulations 1994 (again responding to EU law), and criminal sanctions possibly provide more effective control of defective products;
   - civil liability in the Act is in s2(1) 'where any damage is caused wholly or partly by a defect in a product, every person to whom subsection 2 applies shall be liable …'.

Who can be sued under the Act

1. Potential defendants are listed in s2(2).
   a) Producers – defined in s1(2) and including:
      - the manufacturer, i.e. the manufacturer of the final product; manufacturers and assemblers of component parts; and also producers of raw materials;
      - a person who 'wins' or 'abstracts' products, e.g. someone who extracts minerals from the ground;
      - a person carrying out an industrial or other process which adds to the essential characteristic of the product, e.g. freezing vegetables.
   b) Importers, suppliers and 'own-branders', also defined in s2(2) and liable to the consumer in certain circumstances:
      - importers (by s2(2)(c) includes anybody who in the course of business imports a product from outside EU;
      - suppliers (retailers or equivalent, usually only liable in contract law, but by s2(3), where it is impossible to identify a 'producer' or importer, supplier is liable if consumer asked supplier to identify producer, within a reasonable time of the damage suffered, because it is impractical for consumer to identify producer, and

supplier has failed to identify or refuses to identify it
(so businesses must keep records of their suppliers);
- own-branders (by s2(2)(b) these are, for example,
  supermarket chains who, while not producers, hold
  themselves out as producers by declaring a product as
  their own brand. They must indicate that someone else
  is producing the goods for them in order to avoid
  liability under the Act.

2. Anyone in chain of manufacture and distribution is
   potentially liable.
   - Liability is joint and several, so consumer can sue the
     person with the most money or best insurance cover.
   - Liability is strict so fault need not be proved.

Products covered by the Act

1. Product is defined in s2(1) as 'any goods or electricity and
   (subject to subsection (3)) includes a product which is
   comprised in another product, whether by virtue of being a
   component part, raw material or otherwise …'.
2. Goods are defined in s45(1) as 'substances, growing crops,
   and things comprised in land by virtue of being attached to it
   and any ship, aircraft or vehicle …'.
3. Certain things are exempted from the scope of the Act:
   - buildings (because they are immovable (though building
     materials can fall within the Act);
   - nuclear power;
   - agricultural produce which has not undergone an
     industrial process – the problem being what is an
     industrial process, e.g. butchery in the light of the BSE
     and CJD problems.

Defects covered by the Act

1. Defect is defined in s3(1) as 'if the safety of the product is not
   such as persons generally are entitled to expect, taking into
   account all the circumstances …'.

2. Courts take into account various circumstances to define safety:
   - manner in which and purposes for which product has been marketed, its get-up, use of any mark in relation to the product and any instructions, or warnings to do or refrain from doing anything in relation to the product;
   - what can reasonably be expected to be done with the product;
   - time when product was supplied by its producer to another.
3. Market can be important (e.g. toys and children) as can use of warnings, so the way the consumer uses the product can relieve liability (e.g. fireworks not to be used indoors).
4. Defects in production or design which render the product unsafe will result in liability under the Act, but the consumer may cause the damage by improper use.
5. Time can be another important factor because knowledge is always increasing. So, if knowledge has changed should a producer recall all products sold however long ago in the past.

Types of damage the Act applies to

1. The Act covers death, personal injury, and loss or damage to property caused by unsafe products.
2. Some limitations are put on this, so no damages possible for:
   - small property damage under £275, so a consumer would need to use contract law;
   - business property, so property must be intended for private use, occupation or consumption;
   - loss or damage to the defective product itself.

Limitation

1. Claimant must begin proceedings within three years of becoming aware of the defect, damage or identity of the defendant or, if damage is latent, the date of knowledge of the claimant provided that is within the ten-year period.

2. Court has discretion to override three-year period in personal injury.

3. In all cases there is an absolute cut-off point for claims of ten years from the date that the product was supplied.

Defences

1. Defences are contained in s4 of the Act, including:
   - compliance with statutory or EU obligations, so defect is an inevitable consequence of complying with law, e.g. a chemical ingredient required by law which turns out to be dangerous;
   - defect did not exist when supplied by the defendant, including, for example, animal rights campaigners 'doctoring' baby food, or defect arises in subsequent product but was not in component;
   - product was not supplied in the course of a business;
   - defendant can show (s)he did not actually supply the product;
   - state of technical or scientific knowledge at relevant time was not such that defendant could be expected to have discovered the defect (*Roe v Minister of Health* (1954)) (this precedes the Act but makes same point). This is controversial and inconsistent with other EU countries, which follow the Directive's wording of when the product was put into circulation.

Some criticisms of the Act

1. The Act is a step forward in a few ways:
   - it has put producers on their guard, and increased knowledge of the need for appropriate checking and quality control;
   - as a result there is a greater likelihood of product recall;
   - it gives consumers more chance of an action because they have a greater range of potential defendants to choose from.

2. However, the Act has several shortcomings:

- it does not apply to all products, or all defects, or all damage;
- the limitation period is very strict;
- the Act does not apply to products supplied before 1988;
- the number of defences make it hard for claimants to succeed;
- causation is still a requirement and the standard of care is very similar to negligence, making it too similar to negligence, and not enough like strict liability which it is supposed to be.

CHAPTER 8

TRESPASS TO THE PERSON

Assault
- Intentionally and directly causing the victim to fear an imminent battery, so based on impression caused rather than what defendant will actually do.
- Can be threatening behaviour (*Read v Coker*)
- Can be a prevented battery (*Stephens v Myers*).
- Words traditionally insufficient without gestures:
  i) can disprove assault (*Tuberville v Davage*);
  ii) words can be duress in contract law (*Barton v Armstrong*);
  iii) now words are enough for assault in crime (*R v Ireland*), (*R v Burstow*).
- Defences are consent, necessity, and self-defence.

Battery
- Intentional, direct, unlawful physical contact with the claimant's body.
- If contact is not intentional then negligence appropriate (*Letang v Cooper*).
- Requires direct contact, but indirect has been accepted in the past (*Gibbons v Pepper, Nash v Sheen*), even where another party makes contact (*Scott v Shepherd*).
- There is some controversy over whether hostility is required – compare (*Wilson v Pringle*) with (*Collins v Wilcock*).
- Medical treatment without consent is battery (*Re F*) but consent need not be informed (*Sidaway v Governors of Bethlem & Maudsley Hospitals*).
- Defences include:
  i) consent (*Simms v Leigh RFC*);
  ii) necessity (*Leigh v Gladstone*);
  iii) self-defence (*Revill v Newbury*);
  iv) inevitable accident (*Stanley v Powell*);
  v) lawful arrest.

TRESPASS TO THE PERSON

False imprisonment
- Requires total bodily restraint (*Bird v Jones*).
- No action possible if a means of escape exists (*Wright v Wilson*).
- Liability possible where claimant unaware of the restraint (*Meering v Graham White Aviation*).
- No liability merely because claimant must pay to escape (*Robinson v Balmain Ferry*).
- No liability where employer has legitimate expectation that employee will complete shift (*Herd v Weardale Steel, Coal and Coke*).
- Defences include: consent, mistaken arrest, lawful arrest – and rules on arrest apply.

8.1 ASSAULT

8.1.1 Definitions

1. The old view was that assault was an incomplete battery.
2. Modern definition is intentionally and directly causing a person to fear being victim of an imminent battery (*Letang v Cooper* (1965)).

8.1.2 Ingredients of the tort

1. Assault is free-standing, so intention refers to the impression it will produce in claimant, not as to what defendant intends to do. Compare (*R v St. George* (1840)) with (*Blake v Barnard* (1840).
2. No harm or contact is required (*I de S et Ux v W de S* (1348)).
3. Requires active behaviour, so merely barring entry is no assault (*Innes v Wylie* (1844)).
4. However, threatening behaviour can be assault (*Read v Coker* (1853)).
5. An attempt to commit a battery which is thwarted is still an assault (*Stephens v Myers* (1830)).
6. Traditionally words alone were not an assault:
   - but could disprove an assault (*Tuberville v Savage* (1669));
   - and a threat on its own can be assault (*Read v Coker*);
   - and in contract law, words can amount to duress if the threat is sufficiently serious (*Barton v Armstrong* (1969));
   - more recently, in crime, words alone and even silence have been accepted as assault (*R v Ireland; R v Burstow* (1998)).
7. The claimant must be fearful of an impending battery. Compare *Smith v Superintendent of Woking* (1983)) with (*R v Martin* (1881)).

8.1.3 Defences

1. Consent (as in sports).
2. Self-defence (e.g. threatening an attacker).

3. Necessity (frightening people away from possible harm).

8.2 BATTERY

8.2.1 Definitions

There are a number of possible definitions :

- the defendant intentionally and directly applies unlawful force to claimant's body – but force is irrelevant in, for example, medicine;
- the defendant, intending the result, does an act which directly and physically affects the claimant, but still implies damage;
- has been said to include the 'ordinary collisions of life', but this is very unlikely (*Wilson v Pringle* (1987)).

8.2.2 Ingredients of the tort

1. Intention is a fairly recent requirement – without it an action should be brought in negligence (*Fowler v Lanning* (1959)).

2. Traditional distinction was between direct and indirect contact:

- but now between intention and negligence (*Letang v Cooper* (1965));
- although in traditional cases indirect damage was often accepted (*Gibbons v Pepper* (1695));
- often where negligence might have seemed more appropriate (*Nash v Sheen* (1953));
- and even where other parties have actually caused the harm (*Scott v Shepherd* (1773)).

3. Usually no liability for omissions in trespass, only positive acts (*Fagan v Metropolitan Police Commissioner* (1969)).

4. Hostility is a recent requirement, with traditional foundations

- Lord Holt C.J. in *Cole v Turner* (1704)) suggested that 'the least touching of another in anger is a battery ...';
- restated in *Wilson v Pringle* (1987));

- but conflicting with Lord Goff's test in (*Collins v Wilcock* (1987)) of whether the contact is acceptable in the conduct of daily life.
5. Medical treatment without consent has always been battery:
    - a view reaffirmed by Lord Goff in (*Re F* (1990));
    - and in *T v T* (1988) the court refused to follow (*Wilson v Pringle*);
    - so consent is clearly an issue in medical treatment, but it is arguable what level of information is required for consent to be valid (*Sidaway v Governors of Bethlem Royal and Maudsley Hospitals* (1985));
    - and patients are more likely to sue in medical negligence than in battery, according to the basic principle in (*Bolam v Friern Hospital Management Committee* (1957)).

8.2.3 Defences

1. *Volenti non fit injuria* – consent:
    - in legitimate sporting injuries (*Simms v Leigh RFC* (1969));
    - but not if inflicted outside proper rules (*Condon v Basi* (1985));
    - in medical treatment consent invalid if patient is not broadly aware of type of treatment, etc. (*Chatterton v Gerson* (1981));
    - if the patient is informed of the type of treatment but not the true extent of the risk there is no liability since English law has no doctrine of informed consent (*Sidaway v Governors of Bethlem Royal and Maudsley Hospitals* (1985)).
2. Necessity: justified if it is to prevent greater harm, e.g. death (*Leigh v Gladstone* (1909)).
3. Self-defence:
    - only if reasonable force used (*Lane v Holloway* (1968));
    - a trespasser may defeat the defence where unreasonable force is used against him (*Revill v Newbury* (1996)).
4. Parental chastisement:
    - a traditional right of parents to punish their naughty children;

- without reasonable force it may be tortious;
- it may not in any case have survived the Children Act.
5. Inevitable accident: possible if injury is unavoidable and beyond defendant's control (*Stanley v Powell* (1891)).
6. Lawful ejectment of a trespasser: depends on using reasonable force (*Revill v Newbury* (1996)).
7. Lawful arrest:
   - by a police officer under ss24 and 25 PACEA;
   - by a citizen subject to the common law rules;
   - in either case the arrest must be by reasonable force.

8.3 FALSE IMPRISONMENT

8.3.1 Definition and ingredients of the tort

1. This tort is committed where the defendant imposes intentionally and directly a total restraint on the liberty of the claimant.
2. It is usually associated with wrongful arrests in the modern day, either by police or by security guards, store detectives, etc.
3. The restraint must be total (*Bird v Jones* (1845)).
4. The extent of the restraint could be large, but not, for example, a country.
5. No action if a means of escape exists (*Wright v Wilson* (1699)).
6. The restraint must be directly applied, but if it is not an action is still possible in negligence (*Sayers v Harlow UDC* (1958)).
7. There may even be liability where the claimant is unaware of the restraint (*Meering v Graham White Aviation* (1919)).
8. Or even if claimant is unconscious (*Murray v MOD* (1988)).
9. Not actionable merely because claimant is obliged to pay to get free, where he is contractually bound by a voluntary arrangement (*Robinson v Balmain New Ferry Co.* (1910)).
10. Not actionable if an employer legitimately expects an employee to stay till end of shift (*Herd v Weardale Steel, Coal and Coke Co.* (1915)).

11. It is an unlawful arrest which is made for a purely civil offence (*Sunbolf v Alford* (1838)).

12. It is false imprisonment to keep a prisoner past the lawful release date (*Cowell v Corrective Services Commissioner* (1989)) and *R v Governor of Brockhill Prison ex parte Evans* (2000)).

13. But less convincingly false imprisonment where prisoners are maintained in a condition at odds with the prison rules. See the debate between CA in (*Wheldon v Home Office* (1990)) and DC in (*R v Deputy Governor of Parkhurst Prison* (1990)).

8.3.2 Defences

1. *Volenti non fit injuria* – consent, e.g. lawyer locked in cell with client.

2. Mistaken arrest – available to police only, if they act reasonably.

3. Lawful arrest:
   - powers defined in Police and Criminal Evidence Act 1984;
   - a police officer can arrest on suspicion;
   - private citizens (security guards, store detectives) must be sure an arrestable offence has been or is being committed.

4. There are also common law rules on arrest.
   - An arrest must be made using reasonable force (*Treadaway v Chief Constable of the West Midlands* (1994)).
   - The arrest must not itself be an actionable trespass (*Hsu v Commissioner of the Police of the Metropolis* (1996)).
   - The person must be informed of reasons for arrest (*Christie v Leachinsky* (1947)).
   - In citizen's arrest the person must be taken to a police station within reasonable time (*John Lewis & Co. v Tims* (1952)) (or in arrest by police as soon as is reasonably practicable.
   - An unreasonable period of detention can be as little as 15 minutes (*White v WP Brown* (1983)).
   - PACEA (1984) includes a code of conduct for police.

5. So arrest or detention should not offend the codes of practice or in any way be oppressive.

8.4 INTENTIONAL INDIRECT HARM

1. Originally if trespass was unavailable a novel action was needed.
2. To get over the problem of harm being direct rather than indirect courts accepted other principles:
   - a duty not to deliberately cause harm (*Bird v Holbrook* (1828));
   - an action for indirect but intentional harm (1828); *Wilkinson v Downton* (1897); and *Janvier v Sweeney* (1919)).
3. Negligence now applies to most actions not covered by trespass.

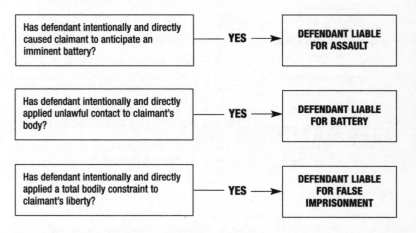

The different ways of committing trespass to the person

CHAPTER 9

TORTS AFFECTING REPUTATION

Classifications

Libel:
- permanent form, e.g. in writing, but also films (*Youssoupoff v MGM Pictures*);
- wax effigy (*Monson v Tussauds*);
- actionable *per se*.

Slander:
- transitory form, e.g. spoken;
- requires proof of damage unless suggesting:
  i) an offence involving prison;
  ii) a contagious disease;
  iii) unchastity of women;
  iv) incompetence in a trade, profession or employment.

DEFAMATION

Ingredients of the tort:

Publication:
- Involves making statement to a third party.
- So includes when defendant knows that someone other than claimant will open a letter (*Theaker v Richardson*).
- And things like graffiti (*Byrne v Deane*).
- But not where claimant shows a letter to a third party (*Hinderer v Cole*).
- Nor remarks in a sealed letter (*Huth v Huth*).

Of a defamatory statement:
- Judge decides whether statement is capable of being defamatory and jury whether it is in fact.
- Must lower esteem of claimant in the minds of right thinking people (*Sim v Stretch*).
- Can be any derogatory remarks (*Cornwell v Daily Mail*).
- Or can be by innuendo (*Monson V Tussauds* and *Tolley v Fry*).
- But not if implying honesty (*Byrne v Deane*).

Referring to the claimant:
- False statement must refer to claimant
- Which may even be through a fictional name (*Hulton v Jones*).
- But cannot include a class that is too broad and vague (*Le Fanu v Malcolmson*).

Defences

Justification:
- the truth can never be defamatory;
- burden is on defendant to show statement is true (*Archer v The Star*);
- can be complex where general rather than specific allegations made (*Bookbinder v Tebbitt*).

Fair comment:
- protects press freedom where comment is of public interest (*London Artists v Litter*);
- defence can fail if malice proved (*Thomas v Bradbury Agnew & Co*).

Absolute privilege:
- applies in Parliament and court and fair reporting of either, and to client.

Qualified privilege:
- applies to memos, references, reports on Parliament not in Hansard;
- can be defeated if malice shown.

Unintentional defamation:
- where defendant does not know of defamation – now in ss2–4 1996 Act.

Innocent dissemination:
where defamation repeated innocently (*Vizetelly v Mudies Select Library*).

Volenti:
where defendant has in effect invited publication (*Moore v News of the World*).

9.1 DEFAMATION

9.1.1 The categories of defamation

1. The main tort developed to protect reputation.
2. As such it can be made in a number of ways, but there are two specific categories: libel and slander.
3. The general distinction is between 'permanent' and 'transitory':
   - libel has been called a written form and slander a spoken form;
   - this view is no longer adequate because of modern technology;
   - the difference owes more to origins than real justification;
   - it has been discarded by most commonwealth jurisdictions;
   - this was recommended in the UK by the Faulkes Report;
   - but the Defamation Act 1996 did not address this issue.
4. The two categories do have two important distinctions:
   a) Libel can be crime as well as tort (*R v Lemon* (1977)).
   b) Libel is actionable *per se*; for slander damage must be shown, except in four circumstances:
      - imputation of an offence involving imprisonment;
      - imputation of a contagious disease;
      - imputation of 'unchastity' of women (Slander of Women Act 1891), including lesbianism (*Kerr v Kennedy* (1942));
      - imputation of unfitness or incompetence in a trade, profession, office or calling (and now by Defamation Act 1952 for any employment provided claimant could be harmed as a result.
5. The difference between permanent and transitory is not always obvious, but there are acknowledged situations:
   - a written defamation is obviously libel;
   - films are libels (*Youssoupoff v MGM Pictures Ltd* (1934));
   - radio and television broadcasts are libel under the Defamation Act 1952 and the Broadcasting Act 1990;
   - by the Theatres Act 1968 s4 a defamation in a public performance of a play is also libel;

- wax effigy in a museum is libel (*Monson v Tussauds* (1894));
- a red light hung outside a woman's house could be libel;
- the spoken word in general is slander;
- gestures in general are slander;
- tapes are probably slander because they can be wiped;
- but other recordings, such as CD and vinyl, whether made in studios or from live performance, are less easy to categorize.

9.1.2 The definition and ingredients of the tort

Definition

1. Defined as 'the publishing of a defamatory statement which refers to the claimant and which has no lawful justification …'.
2. Each separate element of the tort must be proved

Publication

1. This involves communicating the statement to a third party.
2. Each repeat is a fresh publication and therefore actionable, so there can be many defendants to a defamation action.
3. Publication could include:
   - a postcard (as it is assumed it will be seen by a third party);
   - every sale of a newspaper;
   - every lending of a book from a library;
   - a letter addressed to the wrong person;
   - a letter the defendant knows someone besides the claimant might open (*Pullman v Hill* (1891)) and (*Theaker v Richardson* (1962));
   - graffiti that cannot be removed (*Byrne v Deane* (1937));
   - making a remark so that it is overheard;
   - the defendant can also be liable for the consequences of a defamatory statement that (s)he knows will be repeated (*Slipper v BBC* (1991));

- it is uncertain whether repeating the remark through internal mail amounts to fresh publications.

4. In the following there is generally no publication:
- a statement made only to the claimant who then shows it to a third party (*Hinderer v Cole* (1977));
- communication between spouses only;
- a letter addressed only to the claimant;
- remarks contained in a sealed letter (*Huth v Huth* (1915));
- an 'innocent dissemination' (*Vizetelly v Mudies Select Library Ltd* (1900)).

The defamatory statement

1. Defamation trials involve a jury.
2. The judge directs the jury on the meaning of defamation.
- If the judge concludes that no reasonable man could find the words defamatory (s)he withdraws the case from the jury (*Capital & Counties Bank Ltd v Henty* (1882)).
- If the meaning can only be defamatory the jury is so directed.
3. If more than one defamatory meaning is alleged the judge rules which words are capable of being defamatory and which to put before the jury (*Lewis v Daily Telegraph* (1964)).
- In *Mapp v Newsgroup Newspapers Ltd* (1997) CA held that the judge should evaluate the words to delimit the possible range of meanings.
- By s7 Defamation Act 1996 either party can ask before trial if words are capable of bearing a particular meaning.
4. The jury then decides whether the words in fact are defamatory: 'a statement which tends to lower the plaintiff in the minds of right-thinking members of society generally, and in particular to cause him to be regarded with feelings of hatred, contempt, ridicule, fear and disesteem …' (Lord Atkin in *Sim v Stretch* (1935)).
5. So defamatory remarks depend entirely on context and include:
- vulgar abuse (*Cornwell v Daily Mail* (1989)); derogatory

remarks (*Savalas v Associated Newspapers* (1976)) and
Roach v Newsgroup Newspapers Ltd (1992));
- references to a person's moral character (*Stark v Sunday People* (1988)).

6. Implying honesty is not defamatory (*Byrne v Deane* (1937));
nor are statements that lead to sympathy rather than scorn
(*Grappelli v Derek Block Holdings Ltd* (1981)).

7. 'Innuendo' can also be defamation:
- so, words can defame because of their juxtaposition with other things (*Monson v Tussauds* (1894)) and (*Cosmos v BBC* (1976));
- or by containing hidden meaning (*Tolley v Fry & Sons Ltd* (1931)) and (*Cassidy v Daily Mirror* (1929));
- although a complaint of such a meaning can bring other evidence into court (*Allsopp v Church of England Newspaper Ltd* (1972)).

Referring to the claimant

1. The claimant must show that the statement referred to him/her:
- this is easy if (s)he is named:
- it is sufficient if claimant can show people might think it refers to him/her;
- this may be shown even if a fictional name is used (*Hulton & Co. v Jones* (1910));
- or if two people have the same name (*Newstead v London Express Newspapers Ltd* (1940));
- or with cartoons (*Tolley*).

2. Vague generalisation about a broad class are difficult to relate to a particular claimant.
- Class defamation is possible if a claimant can show (s)he is identifiable as a member of the class. Compare (*Knupffer v London Express Newspapers Ltd* (1944)) with (*Le Fanu v Malcolmson* (1848)).

9.1.3 Defences

Without lawful justification
1. 'Without justification' refers to the existence or not of a defence.
2. Traditional common law defences have been added to by statute.
3. Each is complex and usually applies in specific circumstances.

Justification
1. This is a complete defence, since truth can never be defamatory.
2. It is not straightforward because the burden of proof is on the defendant to show that the allegation was true (*Archer v The Star* (1987)).
3. Problems arise where the defendant makes a general rather than a specific allegation (*Bookbinder v Tebbitt* (1989)).
4. By s5 Defamation Act 1952 the defence will not fail 'by reason only that the truth of every charge is not proved …'.
5. However, there are important exceptions to this principle (*Charleston v Mirror Group* (1996)).
6. Possible on revealing spent conviction if no malice is shown.

Fair comment
1. Protects the right to express opinions, e.g. freedom of the press so sometimes called the 'critics defence'.
2. It only applies where the comment is of public interest (*London Artists Ltd v Littler* (1969)).
3. The opinion must be based on facts (*Kemsley v Foot* (1952)).
4. The defendant need not show an honest belief if the comment is 'fair' by an objective test (*Telnikoff v Matusevitch* (1992)).
5. By s6 Defamation Act 1952 the defence does not fail merely because 'the truth of every allegation of fact is not proved …'.
6. However, the defence can be defeated by proof of malice (*Thomas v Bradbury, Agnew & Co. Ltd* (1906)).

Absolute privilege

1. In certain situations freedom of speech is essential.
2. These are given absolute protection of the freedom and include:
   - statements made in either House of Parliament (Bill of Rights 1688) can now be waived under s13 Defamation Act 1996;
   - official reports of parliamentary proceedings, i.e. Hansard;
   - judicial proceedings (which covers judge, jury, lawyers, parties, and witnesses, but not the public (*Mahon and another v Rahn and others* (2000));
   - 'fair, accurate and contemporaneous' reports of judicial proceedings (s3 Law of Libel Amendment Act 1888 for the press and now s9(2) Defamation Act 1952 for broadcasters);
   - communications between lawyer and client;
   - communications between officers of state.

Qualified privilege

1. This is complex and different to absolute privilege since it concerns the communication itself, rather than the occasion when it is made.
2. So it can be defeated by showing malice. Compare *Horrocks v Lowe* (1974)) with (*Angel v Bushel Ltd* (1968)).
3. But it applies in a number of situations:
   - in exercise of a duty, e.g. a comment made in a reference;
   - in protecting an interest, e.g. a comment made in internal memos within a business;
   - in the fair, accurate and contemporaneous reports of parliamentary proceedings, i.e. not in Hansard (*Reynolds v Times Newspapers* (1998));
   - in fair reporting of judicial proceedings (under the Defamation Act 1996 this includes all court and official proceedings or official proceedings world wide;
   - in fair and accurate reporting of public meetings (*Turkington and others v Times Newspapers* (2000));

- a complex list under s7 Defamation Act 1952 also includes:
    (i) those privileged without an explanation under Part 1 of the Schedule, e.g. public proceedings in Commonwealth Parliaments;
    (ii) those privileged subject to an explanation under Part 2 of the Schedule, e.g. fair and accurate reports of trade associations.

  N.B. in either case if malice is proved it defeats the defence

Unintentional defamation

1. This applies under s4 Defamation Act 1952 where a defendant is unaware of the defamatory nature of remarks made.
2. It remedies situations like those in *Hulton* and *Cassidy*.
3. The statement must have been innocently made.
4. Defendant may offer amends by suitable apology, payment into court, supported by affidavit saying why publication was innocent:
   - if accepted there can be no further action;
   - if not the defendant may still have a defence if (s)he shows:
       (i) publication was innocent and no negligence in making it;
       (ii) offer of amends was made as soon as possible;
       (iii) the statement was made without malice.
5. The defence was criticised by the Faulkes Committee.
6. Now under ss 2–4 Defamation Act 1996 there is a rebuttable presumption of innocent publication

Innocent dissemination

Protects producers of mechanical reproduction or distribution if they can show that:
   - they were innocent of knowledge of the defamation;
   - there was nothing to alert them to the defamation;
   - their ignorance of the defamation was not negligence.

Volenti non fit injuria

1. Consent to the publication may defeat a claim.
2. It may apply because claimant has passed material on (*Hinderer v Cole*).
3. It may apply because claimant has invited publication (*Moore v News of the World* (1972)).

Accord and satisfaction

Applies if the claimant gives up the right to sue in return for a payment and/or apology.

9.1.4 Remedies

Injunctions

1. Interim injunctions are granted to prevent publication/broadcast.
2. However, this is often accused of 'gagging' free speech.

Damages

1. There are three types in defamation actions:
   - **nominal:** if case is proven but little or no damage is suffered;
   - **contemptuous:** awarded where, even though the claimant wins the case, the jury feel the action should not have been brought (*Dering v Uris* (1964)), where damages of $^1/_2$d were awarded;
   - **exemplary:** used to punish defendant, so damages high.
2. The main criticisms of damages are:
   - that juries award them at all;
   - that judges in other civil actions (e.g. personal injury) are restrained in the damages they may award;
   - that juries are inconsistent in their awards and award excessive sums (*Lord Aldington v Tolstoy and Watts* (1989)) (£1,500,000); (*Donovan v Face* (1992)) (£100,000 damages nearly ruined the magazine);

- now overlarge sums can be reduced, e.g. (*Sutcliffe v Private Eye* (1989)), where damages of £650,000 were reduced to £6,000.

9.1.5 Reform and the Defamation Act 1996

1. The Faulkes Committee in 1975 suggested many reforms:
   - ending the distinction between libel and slander;
   - altering the defence of justification to one of truth;
   - improving the defence of fair comment so it only fails if the comment is not actually a true opinion;
   - qualified privilege to be defeated if the maker takes advantage of the privilege rather than only if there is malice;
   - simplifying the procedural requirements for unintentional defamation;
   - making exemplary damage awards impossible;
   - allowing actions for defaming the dead;
   - reducing the limitation period to three years;
   - making legal aid available;
   - giving judges the responsibility for awarding damages.
2. Later suggestions for simplified procedures have followed.
3. The Defamation Act 1996 attempted to partly reform the law, but is fairly minimal in the reforms it did make, which include:
   - creating a new fast-track system for claims under £10,000 to dispose quickly of small cases;
   - introducing a new 'offer of amends' defence for newspapers in the case of unintentional defamation;
   - certain cases to be heard by a judge alone;
   - reducing the limitation period to one year.

9.1.6 Justifications and criticisms of the tort

1. Justified because we are each entitled to protect our reputation.

2. However, this right must be balanced with freedom of speech:
- so the truth, however damaging, must not be suppressed;
- but the common criticism of defamation law is that it does so.

3. The UK has been very out of line with human rights principles:
- inconsistent with US law – 1st amendment to the constitution;
- out of line with A10 European Convention of Human Rights 'Everyone has the right to freedom of expression. This right shall include freedom to hold opinions and to receive information and ideas without interference by public authority and regardless of frontiers.'
- this was recognised before incorporation by Human Rights Act 1988 (*Rantzen v Mirror Group Newspapers* (1996));
- but the Act should remedy this.

4. It also favours the rich since legal aid is unavailable.
- this can be avoided by bringing an action under malicious falsehood (*Joyce v Sengupta* (1993));
- costs are very prohibitive (*Taylforth v Metropolitan Commissioner & The Sun Newspaper* (1994));
- as a result actions always seem to involve the press and the famous.

5. The defence of privilege can also cause practical problems, but these can be overcome by claiming negligence instead (*Spring v Guardian Assurance plc* (1994)).

6. The use of juries is also criticised:
- their awards are inconsistent and excessive;
- but they are the right body to determine what is in the minds of 'right thinking people';
- and under s8 CLSA CA can now reduce excessive awards.

7. The law also fails to protect the dead whose actions die with them.

9.2 MALICIOUS FALSEHOOD AND DECEIT

The ingredients of deceit

Defendant makes a false statement:
- so it must be a statement of fact, not opinion (*Bisset v Wilkinson*);
- but can be failing to correct a true statement that becomes false (*With v O'Flanagan*).

Defendant knows that the statement is false:
- so makes the statement deliberately, or without belief in its truth, or reckless as to its truth (*Derry v Peek*);
- and an employer can be vicariously liable for the false statements of his employee, or a principal for those of his agent.

Defendant intends claimant to act upon the statement:
- which must be by the person defendant intends (*Peek v Gunley*);
- though the statement need not be made to the claimant (*Langridge v Levy*).

The claimant must rely on the false statement:
- and show detriment by acting on it (*Smith v Chadwick*).

Claimant must suffer damage as a result:
- and can claim for direct consequence loss (*Doyle v Olby (Ironmongers)*).

DECEIT AND MALICIOUS FALSEHOOD

The ingredients of malicious falsehood

Defendant makes a false statement about claimant:
- so it must refer to claimant to be actionable (*Cambridge University Press v University Tutorial Press*).

The statement is made to a third party:
- similar requirement to publication in defamation that claimant's reputation harmed.

The statement is made with malice:
- so must involve absence of just cause or belief (*Joyce v Motor Surveys*).

The statement is calculated to cause damage to claimant:
- so requires specific references to claimant (*White v Mellin*).

Claimant suffers damage or loss:
- which can be general, but must be foreseeable, and special damage need not be proved.

9.2.1 Deceit

1. In deceit a defendant makes a false statement to the claimant, or a class of people including the claimant, knowing it is false, or being reckless, intending that the claimant will rely on it for his conduct, and the claimant does rely on it and suffers damage.
2. A successful claimant can recover for both physical injury and financial loss (*Burrows v Rhodes* (1899)).
3. The tort can also apply to misrepresentations in contract.

9.2.2 The ingredients of deceit

The making of a false statement
1. The false statement must concern a material fact, not a mere opinion (*Bisset v Wilkinson* (1927)).
2. This does not apply if it is based on specialist knowledge (*Esso v Marden* (1976)).
3. It may be a false statement of fact to misrepresent an opinion or knowledge not actually held (*Edgington v Fitzmaurice* (1885)).
4. A false statement includes failing to correct a true statement that becomes false (*With v O'Flanagan* (1936)).

Knowledge that the statement is false
1. The test is in (*Derry v Peek* (1889)), where false statement was made:
   - knowingly; or
   - without belief in its truth; or
   - reckless as to whether it was true or not.
2. If a servant acting in the course of his employment commits deceit then the master is vicariously liable.
3. The same is likely to be true of agents and their principals.

Intention that the statement should be acted upon
1. The defendant must intend the statement to be acted upon.

2. Only people in the class that the defendant intended to act upon the statement can sue (*Peek v Gurnley* (1873)).
3. So the representation need not be made personally to the claimant (*Langridge v Levy* (1837)).
4. The mere fact that it is foreseeable that the claimant may act on the statement is not enough (*Caparo v Dickman* (1990)).

Reliance on the statement

1. The claimant must show detriment caused by acting on the statement (*Smith v Chadwick* (1884)).
2. It need not be the only reason that he acted as he did.

Damage suffered by the claimant

1. The claimant must suffer damage e.g. economic loss, personal injury, property damage, distress (*Archer v Brown* (1984)).
2. Any losses that are a direct consequence of the deceit are recoverable (*Doyle v Olby (Ironmongers) Ltd* (1969)).

9.2.3 Malicious falsehood

1. Also known as injurious falsehood, a generalisation of specific cases (*Ratcliffe v Evans* (1892)) with origins in slander of title – questioning a person's title to land and making it less saleable.
2. In the 19th century it extended to include slander of goods.
3. It now includes protecting personal business interests (*Kaye v Robertson* (1991)) and (*Joyce v Sengupta* (1993)).
4. There must be a false statement about the claimant, made to a third party, and made maliciously, calculated to cause the claimant damage, and actually causing damage to the claimant.

9.2.4 The ingredients of the tort

A false statement about the claimant

1. The statement must be false, so trade puffs are not actionable, but false statements running down competitors' goods may be

(*De Beers Abrasive Products Ltd v International General Electric Co. of New York* (1975)).

2. A statement not referring to the claimant is not actionable even if it causes damage (*Cambridge University Press v University Tutorial Press* (1928)).

A statement made to a third party

1. A similar requirement to publication in defamation.
2. Third parties must be turned off the claimant before he suffers loss.

Malice

1. Claimant must prove that the statement was made with malice.
2. Malice need not necessarily involve dishonesty.
3. It must involve the absence of just cause or of belief in the statement (*Joyce v Motor Surveys Ltd* (1948)).

Calculated to cause damage to the claimant

1. Calculated means foreseeable.
2. So specific references rather than general ones are necessary. Compare (*Lyne v Nicholls* (1906)) with *White v Mellin* (1895)).

Damage suffered by the claimant

1. The claimant must show actual loss.
2. Loss can be general rather than, for example, loss of a specific customer.
3. Damage can include property damage and financial loss.
4. The test for remoteness is foreseeability.
5. The claimant need not prove special damage:
   - if the statement is in written or permanent form and calculated to cause financial loss; or
   - calculated to cause the claimant a financial loss in respect of a claimant's office, profession, calling, trade, or business at the time of publication (s3 (i) Defamation Act (1952).
6. Suing in defamation instead can be advantageous (*Fielding v Variety Incorporated* (1967)).

CHAPTER 10

EMPLOYMENT-RELATED TORTS

Purpose, criticisms
Justified because:
- employer has some control;
- employer selects employee;
- employer can stand loss;
- employer must have public liability insurance;
- ensure claimant has an action.

Criticised because:
- employer liable for something he did not do;
- ignores fault principle.

Testing employee status
Tortfeasor must be employee for employer to be liable.
- originally based on control test (nature and degree of detailed control (*Performing Rights Society v Mitchell*).
- Then based on integration test – more integrated into organisation then more likely to be an employee (*Stevenson, Jordan & Harrison v MacDonald & Evans*).
- And finally based on the economic reality test (*Ready Mixed Concrete v Minister of Pensions*):
  (i) agreement to provide skill for wage;
  (ii) employer exercises degree of control;
  (iii) nothing inconsistent with employment and weigh up all factors, e.g. ownership of tools, payment of tax and NI, method of payment, self-description, etc.
- Some workers not so straightforward, e.g. casual workers (*Carmichael v National Power*), outworkers (*Nethermere (St Neots) v Taverna*).

VICARIOUS LIABILITY

Other liability
Independent contractors, if hired for purpose (*Ellis v Sheffield Gas Consumers*) or non-delegable duty by statute or common law.

Crimes of employees, if part of employment (*Lloyd v Grace Smith*).

For loaned cars, to give claimant a remedy (*Morgans v Launchbury*).

Did tort occur in course of employment?
Employer only liable if tort in course of employment.
In course of employment:
- authorised act (*Poland v Parr*);
- ignore express order (*Limpus v London General Omnibus*);
- carelessly undertakes work (*Century Insurance v Northern Ireland Transport Board*);
- uses unauthorised help (*Rose v Plenty*);
- over-enthusiastic (*Bayley v Manchester, Sheffield & Lincolnshire Railways*).

Not in course of employment:
- act not within scope of employment (*Beard v London General Omnibus*);
- on a frolic (*Hilton v Thomas Burton*);
- giving unauthorised lifts (*Twine v Beans Express*);
- exceeding proper limits of job (*Makanjuola v Metropolitan Police Commissioner*);
- driving to work unless paid to (*Smith v Stages*).

10.1 VICARIOUS LIABILITY

10.1.1 Origins, purposes and criticisms

1. Not a tort, but imposing liability on someone other than tortfeaser.
2. Originally based on the idea of control, which was appropriate to the 19th century master and servant laws.
3. Rarely appropriate now other than to employment.
4. Sometimes criticised for being unfair because:
   - employer is made liable for something he has not done; and
   - it directly contradicts the fault principle.
5. But there are a number of justifications:
   - traditionally an employer did have control;
   - the employer is responsible for choice of staff;
   - the employer is better able to stand any loss, e.g. from profit;
   - employers must in any case insure for public liability;
   - it may be impossible to trace the person actually; responsible (which may be appropriate, e.g. in medical cases).
6. While vicarious liability has been accepted in sexual harassment (*Bracebridge Engineering Ltd v Derby* (1990)) and racial harassment (*Jones v Tower Boot Co. Ltd* (1997)), it has been rejected in claims against councils for physical abuse by carers (*Trotman v North Yorkshire County Council* (1998)), but accepted in claims against education authorities where staff fail to diagnose and make effective provision for special needs such as dyslexia (*Phelps v Hillingdon LBC* (2000)).
7. Liability is only for a tort by an employee acting in the course of employment, so there are three key questions:
   a) Was the person committing the tort an employee?
   b) Was the tort committed in the course of employment?
   c) Was the act a tort?

10.1.2 Was the tortfeaser an employee?

1. There have been numerous methods of testing employment.

2. The original test was the control test from master/servant law:
- a) measured by 'nature and degree of detailed control ...' (*Performing Rights Society v Mitchell* (1924));
- b) four key factors to be considered: selection, wages, control, and dismissal (*Lord Thankerton in Short v Henderson* (1946));
- c) it is sometimes almost impossible to apply, e.g. medicine;
- d) but it may be appropriate to borrowed workers (*Mersey Docks & Harbour Board v Coggins & Griffiths* (1947)).

3. Lord Denning introduced the 'integration' or 'organisation test' in (*Stevenson, Jordan & Harrison v MacDonald & Evans* (1952)) (the more the worker is integrated into the organisation the more likely (s)he is employed) (*Whittaker v Minister of Pensions and National Assistance* (1967)).

4. The modern test is that of Mackenna J. in *Ready Mixed Concrete Ltd v Minister of Pensions* (1968) (the 'economic reality' or 'multiple test':
- three conditions were identified:
  - (i) employee agrees to provide skill in return for a wage;
  - (ii) employer exercises a degree of control;
  - (iii) nothing in terms inconsistent with employment;
- there are many factors to take into account, but are not definitive: ownership of tools, tax and NI liability, method of payment, self-description, etc.

5. Certain types of worker do not conform easily to any test:
- casual workers (*O'Kelly v Trust House Forte* (1983)) and, more recently, (*Carmichael v National Power plc* (2000));
- outworkers (*Nethermere (St Neots) v Taverna* (1984)), usually considered self-employed;
- labour only sub-contractor (*Lane v Shire Roofing Co.* (1996)), usually seen as self-employed;
- hospital workers – compare *Hillyer v St. Bartholomews Hospital* (1909) with *Cassidy Minister of Health* (1951).

10.1.3 Was the act in the course of employment?

1. Generally a question of fact, but based on policy so inconsistent.
2. If the employee commits the tort in the course of employment then the employer can be vicariously liable.
3. If the tort happens outside of the course of employment or the employee is on a 'frolic of his own' the employer is not liable.
4. There is generally said to be liability for:
   (i) authorised wrongful acts; and
   (ii) authorised acts carried out in a wrongful way.
5. Employer is obviously liable for (I) when instructing the employee to act wrongfully, but can also be liable if the employee has implied authority to commit the tort (*Poland v Parr* (1927)).
6. Authorised acts carried out wrongfully include situations where the employee is engaged in his/her own work, but:
   - ignores an express prohibition (*Limpus v London General Omnibus Co* (1862)), which involved racing buses against instructions and injuring a third party;
   - uses an unauthorised method of work (*LCC v Cattermoles (Garages) Ltd* (1953));
   - acts carelessly (*Century Insurance v N. Ireland Road Transport Board* (1942)), where an explosion was caused while delivering petrol after lighting a cigarette;
   - uses unauthorised help (*Rose v Plenty* (1976)), where liability arose because the employer was seen to gain a benefit;
   - causes the tort by excess of enthusiasm (*Bayley v Manchester, Sheffield, & Lincs. Railway* (1873)).
7. Acts that are outside of employment or 'frolics' include:
   - carrying out an act not within the scope of the employee's work (*Beard v London General Omnibus Co.* (1900));

- diverting away from the proper work on 'a frolic' (*Hilton v Thomas Burton (Rhodes) Ltd* (1961));
- giving unauthorised lifts (*Twine v Beans Express* (1946));
- acting in excess of the proper bounds of the work (*Makanjuola v Metropolitan Police Commissioner* (1992)).

8. The tests are confusing because cases with apparently similar facts will differ in whether liability is imposed.

9. An employer can be liable purely because (s)he derives a benefit from the employee's wrongful act (*Rose v Plenty* (1976)).

10. Whether an employer is liable for torts of employees travelling to and from work depends on whether the travel is part of the work or paid for (*Smith v Stages* (1989)).

10.1.4 Liability for the torts of independent contractors

1. Hirer generally not liable, because of the absence of control
2. However, there are possible exceptions:
   a) if employed for the tort (*Ellis v Sheffield Gas Consumers* (1953));
   b) if there is a non-delegable duty by statute, e.g. to provide and ensure wearing of safety equipment;
   c) if there is a non-delegable duty under common law (*Honeywill & Stein v Larkin* (1984)).

10.1.5 Liability for the crimes of employees

1. There is not usually liability for crimes which give rise to civil liability also (*Warren v Henleys* (1948)).
2. Liability is possible where the crime is part of the employment:
   - as in theft (*Morris v Marten* (1966));
   - and fraud (*Lloyd v Grace Smith* (1912)).

10.1.6 The employer's indemnity

1. At common law an employer can recover from an employee under the principle of subrogation (*Lister v Romford Ice & Cold Storage Co.* (1957)).
2. But this can cause problems so insurance companies usually operate a gentleman's agreement.

10.1.7 Vicarious liability of lenders of cars

1. Vicarious liability can result from the lending of cars (*Britt v Galmoye* (1928)).
2. This can be because the lender gains a benefit (*Ormrod v Crossville Motor Co* (1953)).
3. Or it can simply be to ensure that the injured party has a remedy (*Morgans v Launchbury* (1973)).

10.2 EMPLOYERS' LIABILITY

10.2.1 Origins

1. Employment was traditionally seen as a contractual relationship based on freedom of contract, with no remedies available in tort.
2. In the 19th century there were three major barriers to workers' claims:
    - *volenti* – worker was said to consent to the dangers of work;
    - contributory negligence – a complete defence at that time;
    - 'common employment' – no liability if a 'fellow servant' caused the injury.
3. Most industrial safety law developed in statute.
4. Common law was generally hostile to workers.

Aspects of the non-delegable common law duty

Four key elements:

- Must provide competent fellow employees:
  i) must be competent to carry out work (*General Cleaning Contractors v Christmas*);
  ii) and be well behaved (*O'Reilly's case*).
- Must provide safe plant and equipment:
  i) must provide it and maintain it (*Smith v Baker*);
  ii) now superceded by statute and EU law.
- Must provide safe premises, but only need do what is reasonable to make them safe (*Latimer v AEC*).
- Must provide a safe system of work:
  i) both provide system and ensure it is used safely (*Bux v Slough Metals*);
  ii) although employees are expected to be aware of dangers associated with their skill (*Roles v Nathan*).

Duty has now extended to cover preventing psychiatric harm (*Walker v Northumberland CC*).

EMPLOYERS' LIABILITY

Defences

Volenti (consent):

- but only if employee accepts actual risk (*Smith v Baker*);
- unavailable if employee had no choice but accept risk (*Baker v T E Hopkins*);
- possible if employee sole cause of own misfortune (*Ginty v Belmont Building Supplies*).

Contributory negligence:

- rare but damages can be reduced if employee contributes to harm (*Jones v Livox Quarries*);
- even for death (*Davies v Swan Motor Co*);
- and 100% is possible (*Jayes v IMI (Kynoch)*).

Character of the duty:

- duty is entirely non-delegable (*Wilson & Clyde Coal v English*);
- and is to do what is reasonable (*Latimer v AEC*);
- extends to ancillary activities (*Davidson v Handley Page*);
- but not to property (*Deyong v Shenburn*);
- only reasonable trade practices are acceptable (*Cavanagh v Ulster Weaving*);
- employer must take into account possible extent of injury to employee (*Paris v Stepney BC*);
- and can take into account practicality of any precautions (*Charlton v Forrest Printing Ink*);
- duty is to prevent foreseeable accidents (*Bradford v Robinson Rentals*).

5. Eventually the scope of the three defences was reduced:
- after *Smith v Baker* (1891)) *volenti* only available if the claimant freely accepted risk;
- Law Reform (Contributory Negligence) Act 1945 made the defence a partial one, only affecting the amount of damages;
- by (*Groves v Lord Wimbourne* (1898)) the 'fellow servant' rule was not available to breach of statutory duty, and the Law Reform (Personal Injury) Act 1948 abolished the rule.

6. Other major developments included:
a) employers became liable for defective plant and equipment in the Employers Liability (Defective Equipment) Act 1969;
b) the Workmen's Compensation Act 1897 introduced an insurance principle; later applied to all employees in the Employment Liability (Compulsory Insurance) Act 1969;
c) (*Wilson & Clyde Coal v English* (1938)) identified a non-delegable duty of an employer to his employees.

7. Now the area involves common law, statute, and EU law in Directives implemented as 'the six pack' set of Regulations 1992.

10.2.2 The employers' non-delegable duty

1. The duty includes four key elements, but is an expanding area:
- the duty to provide competent fellow employees;
- the duty to provide safe plant and equipment;
- the duty to provide safe premises;
- the duty to provide a safe system of work.

2. Now the duty also extends to protecting the general health and safety of the employee, including psychiatric health

The duty to provide competent fellow employees

1. All employees should be competent to carry out their contractual duties (*General Cleaning Contractors Ltd v Christmas* (1953)).

2. An employer should ensure the good behaviour of staff (*Hudson v Ridge Manufacturing Co.* (1957)), but is not responsible for unknown characteristics (*O'Reilly v National Rail & Tramway Appliances* (1966)).

3. Actions are rare nowadays because the employer is usually caught by vicarious liability, but it is useful when the employee's act causing injury or damage is outside the scope of employment.

The duty to provide safe plant and equipment

1. The duty is not only to provide safe equipment but to properly maintain it (*Smith v Baker* (1891)).

2. An employer can avoid liability if the employee misuses equipment (*Parkinson v Lyle Shipping Co. Ltd* (1964)).

3. The duty is now possibly superseded by the Employers Liability (Defective Equipment) Act 1969, but the Act itself has been subject to conflicting interpretation (*Coltman v Bibby Tankers* (1988)) (compare CA and HL) and (*Knowles v Liverpool Corporation* (1993)).

The duty to provide safe premises

1. The duty is to do what is reasonably practicable to ensure premises are safe (*Latimer v AEC* (1957)).

2. This may include premises other than the employer's (*Wilson v Tyneside Cleaning Co.* (1958)).

3. There may also be liability under the Occupier's Liability Act 1957.

The duty to provide a safe system of work

1. The duty has two key aspects:
   - creating a safe system of work in the first place;
   - ensuring proper implementation of the system.

2. The duty is to provide an effective system to meet the danger (*General Cleaning Contractors Ltd v Christmas* (1953)), so the employer may be liable for a failure to warn of the danger (*Pape v Cumbria CC* (1992)).

3. There is also a duty to ensure the system is carried out (*Bux v Slough Metals* (1974)).

4. Providing a safe system may include the method of using equipment (*Mughal v Renters* (1993)), so employer may need to:
   - train employees to use equipment safely (*Mountenay (Hazzard) v Bernard Matthews* (1993));
   - and rotate work properly (*Mitchell v Atco* (1995)).

5. The system should not cause undue stress to the employee (*Walker v Northumberland CC* (1994)).

6. An employer cannot rely on an unsafe practice merely because it is a common practice (*Re Herald of Free Enterprise* (1989)).

7. Employees may be expected to be aware of risks associated with the work they do (*Roles v Nathan* (1963)).

8. Much of the duty here has probably now been superseded by, e.g. the duty to undertake risk assessment under the 'six pack'.

10.2.3 Developments in the common law duty

1. Judges have recently expanded boundaries of duty to include:
   - a duty to protect an employee's general health and safety (*Johnstone v Bloomsbury Health Authority* (1991));
   - a duty to protect the psychiatric health of the employee (*Walker* following *Petch v Commissioners of Customs and Excise* (1993));
   - a duty not to negligently prepare references for an employee (*Spring v Guardian Assurance* (1995)).

10.2.4 The character of the duty

1. The duty is entirely personal and non-delegable (*Wilson & Clyde Coal v English* (1938)).

2. The duty is only to do what is reasonable, not to provide a guarantee of safety (*Latimer v AEC* (1953)).

3. The duty extends to all reasonable and ancillary activities (*Davidson v Handley Page Ltd* (1945)).
4. The duty does not extend as far as protecting property (*Deyong v Shenburn* (1946)).
5. An employer can only rely on a trade practice that is reasonable (*Cavanagh v Ulster Weaving Co.* (1960)).
6. But an employer should consider the possible extent of the injury (*Paris v Stepney BC* (1951).
7. An employer may take into account the practicality of any precautions (*Charlton v Forrest Printing Ink Co. Ltd* (1978)).
8. The duty is to prevent accidents that are reasonably foreseeable (*Bradford v Robinson Rentals* (1967)), but not unforeseeable (*Doughty v Turner Manufacturing Co. Ltd* (1964)).

10.2.5 Defences

1. *Volenti* (consent).
   - This only has limited use since (*Smith v Baker* (1891)).
   - But it is possible if employee accepts actual risk (*ICI v Shatwell* (1965)).
   - It cannot be claimed where the employee had no choice but to act (*Baker v T E Hopkins* (1959)).
   - By policy unavailable for breach of a statutory duty (*ICI v Shatwell* (1965)).
   - But it is possible if a claimant is the sole cause of his/her own misfortune (*Ginty v Belmont Building Supplies Ltd* (1959)).
2. Contributory negligence.
   - Can be a defence to any of the duties.
   - However, employees are treated more leniently by the courts (*Caswell v Powell Duffryn Collieries* (1940)).
   - This is because the duty is to protect employees from their own carelessness (*General Cleaning Contractors v Christmas* (1953)).
   - Damages are reduced if employees have contributed to their own injuries (*Jones v Livox Quarries Ltd* (1952)).

Nature of liability
- Regulatory statutes sometimes create civil liability as well as imposing criminal sanctions.
- Action for breach of statutory duty similar to negligence, though standard is set by statute and duty sometimes strict.
- Often hard to decide whether statute does create civil action so requires statutory interpretation.

BREACH OF STATUTORY DUTY

Defences
Volenti – available only if:
- claimant's wrongful act puts defendant in breach (*Ginty v Belmont Building Supplies*);
- vicarious liability is an issue (*ICI v Shatwell*).

Contributory negligence:
- reluctantly accepted (*Casswell v Powell Duffryn Colleries*);
- but 100 per cent possible (*Jayes v IMI (Kynoch)*).

Essential elements of liability
Must ask six questions:
Was Act intended to create civil liability?
- Obvious if statute gives guidance, e.g. HASAW 1974.
- But if silent, use test in (*Lonrho v Shell Petroleum*):
  - i) Presume if Act creates obligation enforceable in only one manner then no other;
  - ii) unless obligation benefits a particular class, or creates public right and claimant suffers damage different to rest of public.
- Wording vital (*Monk v Warbey*) and (*Atkinson v Newcastle Waterworks*).

Is claimant owed a duty of care?
- Must show duty owed as individual or as member of class (*Hartley v Mayoh*).
- Must show Parliament intended to create private law rights (*X (Minors) v Bedfordshire County Council*).

Is duty imposed on defendant?
- Must consider precise words of statute (*R v Deputy Governor of Parkhurst Prison ex parte Hague*).
- No duty, no civil liability.

Has defendant breached duty?
- No single standard, so court must construe from words of statute.
- Subject to dictates of policy (*Ex parte Island Records*).
- If specific words used then standard clear (*Chipchase v British Titan Products*.
- 'Must' and 'shall' usually means liability is strict (*John Summers & Sons v Frost*).

Did breach cause damage?
- 'But for test' applies.

Was damage of type contemplated in Act?
- No liability if type of damage not contemplated in statute (*Gorris v Scott*).
- So damage must not be too remote (*Young v Charles Church*).

- This applies even if death resulted (*Davies v Swan Motor Co. Ltd* (1949)).
- One hundred per cent contributory negligence is possible (*Jayes v IMI Kynoch Ltd* (1985)).

10.3 BREACH OF A STATUTORY DUTY

10.3.1 Introduction

1. Many regulatory statutes impose a duty and create civil liability.
2. An action is similar to negligence, but differs in significant ways:
   - the standard of care is fixed by the statute;
   - the duty can be strict, or the burden of proof may be reversed, either being advantageous to a claimant;
   - such statutes are regulatory, so usually impose criminal sanctions, and the existence of civil liability is debatable;
   - in America breach of the statutory duty can be proof of negligence, but in England it is treated as a separate tort.
3. As a result both are commonly pleaded at the same time.
4. Civil liability is more obvious where the Act modifies common law.
5. Other Acts are harder to determine, so the area is dependent on statutory interpretation and so is unpredictable.
6. Industrial safety law is the most common example.
7. A number of questions must be considered.

10.3.2 The essential elements of liability

Is the Statute intended to create Civil Liability?

1. Claimant must show that the Act creates an action for damages.
2. This Is straightforward if the Act gives specific guidance, e.g. Health and Safety at Work etc Act 1974.

3. Problems can occur if the statute is silent on the issue.

4. Courts must always give effect to the intention of Parliament.

5. The modern test is Lord Diplock's in (*Lonrho Ltd v Shell Petroleum Co.* (1982)):

   a) court presumes that if Act creates obligation enforceable only in specific manner, then not enforceable in any other manner;

   b) but there are two exceptions:
      - when an obligation is to benefit a particular class;
      - when provision creates public right but claimant suffers particular, direct, and substantial damage different from the rest of the public.

6. This test is criticised because of two problems:

   a) it gives the court discretion in determining class;

   b) there is no set distinction between a statute creating a public right and one just prohibiting what was formerly lawful.

7. Courts consider various factors in determining Parliament's intent:

   - civil action more likely to be possible if wording precise. Compare (*Monk v Warbey* (1935)) with (*Atkinson v Newcastle Waterworks* (1877));
   - failure to mention a specific penalty (*Cutler v Wandsworth Stadium Ltd* (1949));
   - some groups are well-established classes (*Groves v Lord Wimbourne* (1898));
   - action is more likely with an identifiable group (*Thornton v Kirklees MBC* (1979));
   - there must be a direct link with purpose of statute (*McCall v Abelsz* (1976));
   - the purpose must be for the benefit of that class (*R v Deputy Governor of Parkhurst Prison ex parte Hague* (1992)).

Is the claimant owed a duty of care?

1. Action only succeeds if claimant shows he is owed duty as an individual or as a member of a class (*Hartley v Mayoh & Co.*

(1954)), so an action by a relative might fail (*Hewett v Alf Brown's Transport* (1992)).

2. There is a wide scope for establishing the existence of a duty (*Gardon Cottage Foods v Milk Marketing Board* (1984)) and (*Atkinson v Croydon Corporation* (1938)).

3. But HL has restated the need to show that Parliament intended to create private law rights (*X (minors) v Bedfordshire County Council*); (*M (a minor) v Newham London Borough Council*); (*Keating v Bromley LBC* (1995)).

Is a duty imposed on the defendant?

1. Must consider precise words of statute (*Ex Parte Hague* (1992)).

2. If there is no duty on the defendant there can be no civil action.

Has the defendant breached a statutory duty?

1. No single standard of care, so court must construe statute.

2. Has been subject to inconsistency and the dictates of policy: Lord Denning in *Ex Parte Island Records* (1978): 'you might as well toss a coin in order to decide the cases'.

3. If the words are specific, the standard is self-evident (*Chipchase v British Titan Products Co. Ltd* (1956)).

4. When words like 'must' or 'shall' are used liability is likely to be strict (*John Summers & Sons v Frost* (1955)).

5. But the standard is often vaguely stated (*Brown v NCB* (1962)).

Did the breach of duty cause the damage?

1. Tested similarly to common law negligence by the 'but for' test.

2. Defendant can be liable if duty also to ensure claimant complies with provision (*Ginty v Belmont Building Supplies Ltd* (1959)).

Was the damage of a type contemplated in the Statute?

1. Liability is not possible if the type of damage was not contemplated in the statute (*Gorris v Scott* (1874)).
2. So it must not be too remote (*Young v Charles Church* (1997)).

10.3.3 Defences

1. *Volenti non fit injuria*:
   a) not normally available on policy grounds;
   b) but may be:
      - where the claimant's wrongful act put the defendant in breach (*Ginty* (1959)); or
      - where the claimant tries to claim vicarious liability as an issue (*ICI Ltd v Shatwell* (1965)).
2. Contributory negligence:
   a) only accepted reluctantly as regulations are often meant to protect workers from their own carelessness: 'employees' sense of danger will have been dulled by familiarity, repetition, noise, confusion, fatigue, and preoccupation with work ...' (*Caswell v Powell Duffryn Collieries* (1940));
   b) but it is possible if claimant is genuinely at fault (*Jayes v IMI (Kynoch) Ltd* (1985)).

Purpose and character

Purpose is to put claimant financially in position as if tort had not occurred, so includes an assessment of future loss.

Contempuous (exemplary) damages are only possible where:

- Government servants act oppressively;
- defendant's conduct calculated to profit from tort;
- statute expressly allows, e.g. Copyright Act 1958.

Personal injury and death

PI damages of two types:

- special damages up to date of trial;
- future losses, e.g. loss of earnings, and a sum appropriate to pain, suffering and loss of amenities.

Pain, suffering and loss of amenities is based on a fixed quantum for each injury.

Loss of earnings is calculated by multiplying a multiplicand (claimant's earnings) by a multiplier (a number of years).

Possible also to have interim awards, provisional awards and strict settlements where the claimant's condition may deteriorate.

Death claims are ot two types:

- on behalf of the deceased's estate under Law Reform (Miscellaneous Provisions) Act 1934;
- on behalf of dependents (and including a sum for bereavement) under Fatal Accidents Act 1976.

Injunctions

- Discretionary.
- Usually prohibitory.
- Can be interlocutory or final.

REMEDIES

Economic loss and property damage

Calculated on:

- loss of property;
- cost of transporting replacements;
- loss of foreseeable profit;
- loss of use till replaced;
- reduction in value.

Problems with damages

- Inaccurate, unfair and inefficient.
- Favour rich because of future loss.
- Bereavement is limited to certain relatives and is not given to cohabitees.
- Need to show fault, so claimants who cannot lose.
- Insurance companies dictate outcome.
- Lump sum nature need not benefit claimant.
- Delays in system put many claimants off.
- Claimants get less than their claims are worth in settlements.
- Enforcement proceedings are often needed.
- Costly to run, e.g. Pearson said 85% of claim.

11.1 DAMAGES

11.1.1 The purpose and character of damages in tort

1. The purpose of damages in tort is to put the claimant in the position (s)he would have been in if the tort had not occurred.
   - So at least one element of damages (general damages) is speculative (a prediction of what would have happened.
   - The obvious danger is that the claimant is either under-compensated or over-compensated.
2. So tort damages is an artificial remedy in many situations since it is only a monetary award.
3. There are different types of damages with different effects.

11.1.2 Non-compensatory damages

1. **Nominal damages** can be awarded if there is no actual loss, but a tort has been committed, e.g. trespass to land.
2. **Contemptuous damages** are awarded when the court thinks the action was unnecessary, e.g. with technical defamations.
3. **Exemplary damages** are designed to punish the tortfeasor:
   - common elsewhere, e.g. personal injury actions in USA;
   - but have restricted use in England and Wales;
   - (*Rookes v Barnard* (1964)) identified three possible categories:
     (i) where government servants act in an oppressive arbitrary or unconstitutional manner;
     (ii) where the defendant's conduct is calculated to profit from the tort, e.g. in some libel actions;
     (iii) where statute expressly allows, e.g. Copyright Act 1956.

11.1.3 Economic loss and damage to property damage

1. Usually compensated as 'special damages'.
2. Usually little problem in calculating such losses.
3. With an economic loss the claimant must be restored as closely as possible to the position if the tort had not occurred.
4. Property damage is calculated according to:
   - loss of the property and its value at the time of loss;
   - cost of transporting replacement property if appropriate;
   - loss of reasonably foreseeable profit;
   - loss of use until the time the property is replaced;
   - reduction in value if damaged but not lost, i.e. repair costs.

11.1.4 Damages in personal injury claims

1. This is divided into two groups.
   a) Special damages:
      - this is pecuniary loss up to the date of trial;
      - can include medical care, equipment, loss of earnings, etc.;
      - but only such expenses as the court considers reasonable, so private medical care may well be refused.
   b) General damages or future damages:
      - includes pecuniary losses, e.g. future earnings, medical costs, costs of care and special facilities;
      - and also non-pecuniary loss, e.g. pain, suffering and loss of amenities (and in the case of death, bereavement).
2. Non-pecuniary losses are difficult to quantify:
   - peculiarities might include, for example, a person in a coma will gain no award for pain and suffering;
   - awards are based entirely on arbitrary calculations.
3. Loss of earnings are quantified by multiplying:
   - a **multiplicand** – the claimant's annual net loss (any

earnings less deductions for, for example, private insurance, sick pay or other benefits etc.) by
- a **multiplier** – notional figure representing the number of years the court feels the award should cover (since the award is made as a lump sum and can be invested, the maximum is 18), less deductions for known illnesses which may cause retirement.
4. Interest to trial is payable on all awards of damages.
5. If it is hard to assess extent of injury, or if claimant's condition may deteriorate, a split trial with interim damages in the case of the first, or provisional damages in the case of the second is possible, or a structured settlement.

11.1.5 The effect of death in tort claims

1. If the claimant dies following the tort, to be fair his action survives.
2. There are two possible actions :
   - on behalf of deceased's estate in Law Reform (Miscellaneous Provisions) Act 1934 (similar to a personal injury action;
   - on behalf of dependants (a limited group) in Fatal Accidents Act 1976 – includes losses following death, and bereavement.

11.1.6 Problems associated with damages

1. Tort damages are considered inaccurate, unfair and inefficient.
2. They are unfair because the rich receive better compensation than the poor, because their future damages are higher.
3. Certain damages, e.g. bereavement, are available to a restricted range of claimants only, and the level is set low and is arbitrary.
4. Damages discriminates against claimants unable to show fault.
5. Insurance companies can decide the outcome of actions.
6. The lump sum nature of an award can be detrimental to the claimant and only benefits lawyers.

7. Delay caused by procedure often causes claimants to give up, which is what the Woolf reforms tried to address.
8. In out-of-court settlements claimants can be forced to accept much lower sums than they actually deserve.
9. Claimants may still need to use enforcement proceedings where the defendant does not pay up.
10. The system of compensation is inefficient – the cost of administering the tort system prior to Woolf was 85% of damages gained.

11.2 INJUNCTIONS

1. This is an equitable remedy.
2. It is therefore at the courts discretion and not easy to obtain.
3. The clear purpose in seeking such a remedy is to prevent continuation of the tort, e.g. appropriate to the economic torts.
4. The most common form is prohibitory, i.e. the defendant must refrain from doing something (the tort complained of).
5. An injunction in tort is awarded in one of two ways:
   - interlocutory – an interim measure sought in advance of trial of the issue, e.g. preventing continued repetition of a libel pending trial;
   - final – where all the relief needed is contained in the order itself, e.g. an order against pickets.

11.3 BASIC LIMITATION PERIODS

11.3.1 The purpose of limitation periods

1. Unfair on defendant to leave him too long without suing.
2. Difficulty of preserving evidence.
3. Encourages P to get on with the case.

11.3.2 Basic periods

1. The general period:

- is contained in s2 Limitation Act 1980;
- and is six years from the date on which the action accrues.

2. Damages for personal injury and death:
   - contained in s11 (4);
   - and is three years from the date on which the action accrued or the date of knowledge, whichever is the later;
   - in fatal accidents where death occurs within three years of the accrual, personal representatives have a fresh limitation period running from the date of death or knowledge of the death (s11(5).

3. Latent damage.
   - Here there are different rules under Latent Damage Act 1986.
   - The action must arise from damage which has lain dormant.
   - The period is six years from the date of accrual or three years from the 'starting date' (date of knowledge), with a 15 years 'longstop bar'.

4. Disabilities.
   - If a person suffers a disability in law, e.g. a minor lacking capacity then the disability is taken into account.
   - Time runs from ceasing of disability e.g. a minor time barred at 24.

11.3.3 The date of knowledge in personal injury

1. This is defined in s14.
2. It means knowledge of certain facts, so is the date when:
   - the claimant first knew the injury was significant;
   - the claimant knew the injury was attributable in whole or part to the defendant's act or omission;
   - the claimant first knew the identity of the defendant;
   - the claimant knew facts supporting a claim of vicarious liability.
3. Significant injury is one where the claimant considered it sufficiently serious to justify beginning proceedings against a defendant not disputing liability and who could pay.

4. Knowledge means of facts, not law, which the claimant could discover on his own or with the help of experts.

11.3.4 Power to disapply the limitation period

1. It is an important power of court in s33 in cases of death and personal injury.
2. The court must consider certain factors:
   - the length of and reasons for the claimant's delay;
   - the effect of delay upon the cogency of evidence;
   - the defendant's conduct after the cause of action, e.g. responses to a claimant's reasonable requests for information;
   - the duration of any disability of a claimant arising after accrual;
   - promptness of claimant once aware of possibility of action;
   - steps taken by claimant to gain expert advice, and advice given.

INDEX